Torture: does it work?

Interrogation issues and effectiveness in the Global War on Terror

Yvonne Ridley

Military Studies Press

Military Studies Press
4 Dencora Park
Shire Hill
Saffron Walden
Essex, CB11 3GB
United Kingdom

First published in 2016
Military Studies Press, an imprint of Books Express Publishing

ISBN-13: 978-1-78266-830-5   paperback
ISBN-13: 978-1-78266-829-9   hardback

CONTENTS

ABOUT THE AUTHOR

Yvonne Ridley is a journalist and author whose focus on modern war studies is borne out of her ordeal of being captured by the ruling Taliban in Afghanistan shortly after 9/11. Living in the Scottish Borders, she still goes into conflict zones and has become an authority on the Global War on Terror.

The contents of this book represent many years of research, including a four day visit to Guantanamo Bay. She has interviewed and drawn on the testimonies of victims of torture from 1945 to the present day as well as consulting with serving and retired military and intelligence officers from East to West.

INTRODUCTION

Since the arrival of the War on Terror years at the beginning of the 21st century the issue of torture has become an unlikely topic which has polarized politicians, divided lawyers and focussed the minds of human rights groups and their advocates.

The Bush Administration is often blamed for this phenomenon and must shoulder most of the responsibility for the unleashing of an aggressive, knee-jerk reaction in response to what happened on September 11 2001. The War on Terror was born out of the unprecedented 9/11 terror attacks and was fuelled by a climate of fear and the need for revenge—furthermore, it had no borders and no limits; it was a new kind of conflict against an unconventional enemy.

Goodwill, sympathy and support from around the world were in plentiful supply, along with a coalition of forces wanting to help American allies in their hour of need.

Shortly after that fateful day, members of the Bush Administration, along with military and intelligence chiefs, began actively investigating the deployment of harsh interrogation techniques designed to be used on the newly rounded-up terror suspects, who would be given the legally obscure sobriquet of "unlawful enemy combatants."

One of the first detainees to enter Guantanamo in January 2002 was Saudi-born Shaker Aamer, who was held there for nearly 14 years without charge or trial. He shared his views on the torture he experienced, expressing the opinion that if doctors and psychologists had withdrawn their services, much of the abuse could not have been carried out.

As it was, little opposition arose to the introduction of new interrogation methods proposed during that incendiary period; the American people were still in a collective state of shock and there was little public appetite for dissenting voices. However, less than a decade later, both domestically and overseas, the legality of those techniques was being openly questioned and deemed by some lawmakers to be nothing short of torture.

International goodwill began to wane as awkward questions were asked about the need to hold people without charge or trial in a limbo outside of the legal frameworks.

Such uncomfortable questions about morals and ethics can be evidenced by the conflicting accounts which have since emerged in political memoirs written by leading members of the 9/11 administration, including the US President himself, George W Bush.

While the moral and legal issues continue to be debated in the second decade of the new millennium, this book delves further into the subject of torture to ask a simple but relevant question: Does it actually work? If the answer is in the affirmative there is a need to further examine its deployment to measure, in terms of success, if it has become a useful weapon in today's modern warfare. In other words, can torture produce useful intelligence and can the various methods of inflicting pain on others in exchange for useful information ever be justified?

To take the issue forward it is therefore necessary to examine, in particular, documents and accounts from the salient experiences of those involved in earlier conflicts from the last century, including World War II, Vietnam and the Algeria-France wars.

Since the battle for hearts and minds – both at home and abroad – is crucial in any conflict, the role of the media and journalists also needs to be examined. The evidence collated for this book has been further bolstered by those able to bring their own unique perspectives to bear … the victims of torture themselves, who through their own experiences, real and imagined, can give a truly informed opinion. For perhaps it is they, more than anyone else, who can answer the question if torture really is a useful weapon in the advancement of today's modern warfare in terms of the intelligence it produces, counterbalanced with the unintended consequences of using such techniques.

Recent documents recovered under the Freedom of Information Act in the US and UK are readily available on the subject; in addition formerly classified documents from the National Archives in the UK and political archives have been used to complement library research which encompassed a reading list of more than 80 books on various aspects of the subject.

As prolific as my reading list is, no single book appears to address the issue of quantifying success or failure through the strategic use of torture in today's modern armies. This book cuts through the moral maze as it attempts to answer that question. The truth is, if torture fails to deliver its objective, its use as a military weapon becomes as pointless as a faulty machine gun and is, perhaps, even a liability.

Addressing the question has taken many years and involved travelling to the detention facilities at Guantanamo, looking inside Colonel Muammar Gadaffi's notorious Abu Salim prison in Tripoli as well as the infamous jail at Robben Island near Cape Town, South Africa where Nelson Mandela was once held.

Talking with detainees and former prisoners, victims of torture and their guards has taken me on a dark journey and to places across Europe, the Middle East, Asia and Africa where the secrets of terrible actions are only now beginning to surface. I even returned to the place I was held for eleven terrifying days and ten long nights as a prisoner of the Taliban – the former intelligence headquarters in Jalalabad where I abandoned all hope of surviving.

It was while being held captive by the Taliban that I became preoccupied with the theme of torture during the short days and the long, long nights. My captors thought I was a spy with useful intelligence to share but I was not a high-value detainee, merely a journalist armed with nothing more than a curious mind, a pen and a notepad. How could I convince them otherwise?

This is a dilemma experienced by few people, but the treatment of prisoners over the decades has had much wider repercussions for unwitting citizens, as this book illustrates, because the implementation of torture thousands of miles away in a dark and secret dungeon can have far-reaching consequences years later.

ACKNOWLEDGEMENTS

I am indebted to all who assisted me in my research for this book, especially those who gave up their time to be interviewed, often revisiting harrowing and traumatic experiences by recounting their experiences at Guantanamo, Bagram and Abu Ghraib as well as other dark sites located around the world. Appreciation also goes to some of their former guards who introduced additional and sometimes alternative perspectives. While most agreed to go on the record there were several who, for valid reasons, offered only background briefings and useful corroboration of facts.

Similarly I'm grateful to the many lawyers and human rights advocates, on both sides of the Atlantic who also gave their time and experience to go beyond the headline stories to provide in-depth analysis along with members of the US military who also submitted their thoughts and perspectives on the subject. Very often the latter group find themselves at the sharp end having to represent and/or justify their governments' decisions.

I am particularly indebted to Dr Matthias Strohn and Professor Lloyd Clark from the Department of War Studies at the Royal Military Academy Sandhurst who tutored me through a Modern War Studies research Masters at Buckingham University. Their dogged pursuit for detail and accountability led me to embark on a previously uncharted, personal journey through the territories of French and Greek philosophers including the works of Thomas Aquinas, Carl Von Clausewitz and a host of other works written by senior French military officers. Largely due to their efforts I felt more equipped to experience the thoughts, challenges and frustrations faced by those working in the complex field of counter intelligence.

Of course none of this could have been achieved without the unwavering support and understanding of my husband Samir Asli, daughter Daisy and mother Joyce.

Many thanks also go to publishers Duncan Evans and John Evans, as well as Molly and Jim Cameron whom I've yet to meet but have unstinting admiration for their tireless work, enthusiasm and editing skills.

Tayyibah Hewitt should receive special recognition for her graphics, photography and creative skills. Projecting the contents of this book with one image to use for the jacket was a challenging task which she acquitted with distinction.

And finally, I owe a great deal to my dear friend and mentor Dr Ahmed Moustapha who gave me the vision and encouragement to write this book. His thoughtful words, support and advice were proffered in the cafes and restaurants off Tahrir

Square in Cairo during the early stages of the Arab Spring when the flame of hope for the Middle East shone brightly as ordinary people in the region rose up against their oppressors. May the Arab people one day be free from the tyranny and fear of the dictators who continue to rule them in that troubled region.

1
A Journey into the Darkness

It is impossible to say what triggered the first act of torture and whether it was used out of simple anger, sadistic pleasure, revenge or the desire for information. Written records from more than 3,000 years ago reveal that it was already in common use[1] and has been widely practised by individuals and societies ever since.

By today's standards, the West is far more advanced and civilized as a society but it is a sad fact that some intelligence agencies rely on certain methods of torture. The use of torture even became a serious debating issue in America for Republican candidates contending for the party's nomination for the US presidential elections of 2012, serving to illustrate just how contemporary and controversial the subject remains.[2] Even for President Barack Obama's Democratic administration, which heralded promises of a new dawn, including the shutting down of Guantanamo Bay's notorious prison complex, torture remains an unresolved issue for which there is still no closure.

It could be regarded as an alarming development by modern society's standards that such a subject – once considered the sign of primitive behaviour – is now regarded in some quarters as a vote winner by politicians who endorse its use. But this book will also illustrate how the popular media, including Hollywood, has embedded the concept of torture as an acceptable interrogation method in the public consciousness to the point of almost normalising what is generally regarded as a criminal, medieval act in international law.

In 1948, torture was prohibited by the United Nations;[3] in the 21st century its practice is also considered illegal under the domestic laws of all Western countries. It was declared a serious violation of human rights as outlined within the framework of the UN Human Rights Charter (formally known as the Universal Declaration of Human Rights).

---

1   Vernon, J.: *The Illustrated History of Torture, from the Roman Empire to the War on Terror*, London, Carlton Books, 2011.

2   Editorial: "The Torture Candidates." *New York Times*, November 15 2011, p. A30 (New York Edition).

3   UN, *Universal Declaration of Human Rights*, Article 5, adopted by the UN General Assembly, December 10 1948 (Paris).

While the moral ethics have been exhaustively debated by political leaders, politicians, lawyers, academics, journalists and human rights groups across the globe[4] without reaching a real conclusion, this book intends to examine the effectiveness of torture and the consequences, if any, as a result of the intelligence gained from its use. In other words: Does torture actually work as a method of gaining valuable intelligence in a world where the conventional battlefield is no more?

Criteria to evaluate its effectiveness include short and long-term benefits gained from disseminating information given under duress and any possible disadvantages. For example, some politicians in America obviously thought it could be a vote winner in the 2012 presidential elections whereas the reaction from the wider world could have damaged long-term relations with other countries. In Libya, for instance, officials from the UK and the US experienced the uncomfortable scenario of sitting down on government business with politicians and military leaders who claimed they had been subjected to rendition, torture and interrogation as terror suspects.

Also during one of my many trips to Libya, I was informed that at least one of the security team of Libyans detailed to protect Hillary Clinton, the US Secretary of State at the time, was a former Guantanamo detainee.

Libyans like former dissidents turned political and military figures Sami al-Saadi and Abdul Hakim Belhaj see themselves as having a positive role to play in the future development of their country, yet a few years ago they were viewed as "the enemy" by Western spy agencies who worked closely with Libyan ruler Colonel Muammar Gadaffi.

However, after the dictator's alienation from his Western allies and his downfall, the full extent of Britain and America's espionage roles in his country was exposed as an unintended consequence of the NATO bombing of government buildings. The intelligence headquarters of Gadaffi's regime was reduced to rubble in 2011 by missiles and smart bombs which also managed to blow wide open the locked filing cabinets containing top-secret documents and communications sent from the US Central Intelligence Agency (CIA) and MI6 as well as other Western intelligence agencies. As I walked through the ruins of the Tripoli regime's intelligence HQ there were still scraps of sensitive documents and secret files to be prised from the rubble.

---

4   Ramsay, Maureen. "Can the Torture of Terrorist Suspects Be Justified?" *The International Journal of Human Rights*, vol. 10, no. 2, 2006.

These materials soon found their way into the hands of those who previously said they had been tortured as a direct result of collaboration between Gadaffi and Western intelligence, including the Belhaj and al-Saadi families. The consequences of this unexpected leak has already cost the British taxpayer[5] $3.5 million US dollars in an award to Sami al-Saadi, who accused MI6 of being instrumental in his and his family's kidnapping and rendition to Libya back in 2004. The out-of-court settlement, with no admissions of guilt, brought an end to any potentially embarrassing court hearing which would have involved the full details emerging of how the al-Saadis were forced to board a plane in Hong Kong and then flown to Libya in a joint UK-US-Libyan operation.

Once arriving in Libya the family say they, including their four children, were detained and tortured. The consequences of Britain being found complicit in the rendition and imprisonment of children could not even be contemplated in some parts of Whitehall.

While visiting Tripoli in 2011 I met up with al-Saadi and later Belhaj, who said he and his family were similarly kidnapped, renditioned and tortured in Libya as a result of cooperation by British and Libyan intelligence agencies. Both men showed me copies of the documents which had surfaced during the NATO bombing of the Libyan capital as evidence which appeared to confirm their stories and original suspicions.

While the al-Saadi family settled out of court in the firm belief that their case would never be heard, Belhaj is still insisting on justice through legal action unless an official apology from the UK Government is given to him. This is regarded as extremely unlikely since such an apology would form an admission of guilt by the then Prime Minister Tony Blair and his Foreign Secretary Jack Straw that the British government had been complicit in kidnap, rendition and torture operations.

So sensitive is the issue of torture in Britain that the UK Government has, over the years, released many official and robust denials of complicity in torture during the global war on terror (GWOT). Responding to the al-Saadi settlement, Straw said: *"At all times I was scrupulous in seeking to carry out my duties in accordance with the law, and I hope to be able to say much more about all this at an appropriate stage in the future."*

---

5   Accessed at http://www.bbc.co.uk/news/uk-20715507.

In October 2014, however, Belhaj won the right[6] to sue the British Government and intelligence agencies in the English courts over claims that he was unlawfully abducted and tortured with the involvement of MI6. The former military commander turned politician, who fled the Gadaffi regime in 1998, insists Straw and senior members of the security services were "co-conspirators" in his illegal detention and torture in 2004, when he and his wife were abducted in China and transported via Malaysia to Thailand and finally to Libya.

In addition he says that when he arrived in Libya he was interrogated at least twice by British agents; again, proof of the allegations appears to be contained in classified documents now in his possession. The most damning correspondence is said to be written communications between a senior intelligence officer of the Gadaffi regime, CIA officials and Sir Mark Allen, who was head of counter-terrorism at MI6 at the time.

Lawyers for the Foreign Office argued unsuccessfully that the Belhaj claims could not be heard in a British court on the grounds of an "act of state doctrine," stating that the UK courts could not inquire into what happened because it also involved agents from a foreign state, namely the US.

Belhaj has insisted he will get justice but by the end of 2015 he appeared to be no further forward in his bid to get his case heard in a British court of law. As for the al-Saadi settlement, it is not the first time the UK Government has sanctioned the payout of so-called "hush money"[7] in bids to thwart allegations being laid against its own security and intelligence agencies.

In 2010, ministers authorised a multi-million pound deal in which all of the men from the UK who were held in Guantanamo Bay would receive a tax-free sum. Kenneth Clarke, the Justice Secretary at the time, advised the British Parliament in November 2010 that the settlement was "significant" but could have ultimately cost taxpayers up to £50 million if cases had gone before the courts.

A number of the former detainees, some of whom have spoken and contributed towards this book, still insist that UK intelligence services were complicit in torture before and after they arrived at Guantanamo. This includes testimony from Shaker Aamer who, as the "Last Londoner" to be released from Guantanamo

---

6   Accessed at http://www.independent.co.uk/news/world/middle-east/libyan-dissident-abdul-hakim-belhaj-can-sue-over-claims-of-mi6-torture-and-abduction-9829348.html.

7   Accessed at http://www.bbc.co.uk/news/uk-11762636.

Bay, gave a flurry of media interviews in December 2015 about his experiences of being held for 14 years without trial or charge. The Saudi-born father of four has demanded a full public inquiry into the security services after claiming British intelligence officers were complicit in his detention and torture.

He says British secret service agents were present in Bagram, where he was interrogated after bounty hunters sold him to the Americans in December 2001. Within two months he was rendered to Guantanamo, where he says he was again interrogated in the presence of British agents—claims which have yet to be accepted by UK authorities.

Even if torture was proven to be an effective intelligence gathering tool, it is clear from the British Government's continual strong denials of complicity that it is not something with which any UK Parliament wants to be associated. Such an admission could undermine moral legitimacy and therefore become counterproductive to a military "hearts and minds" campaign, not only at home, but in areas of conflict where the military is operating today and perhaps in the future.

Certainly subsequent US administrations appear to be wrestling with similar challenges which have already prompted considerable compensation payouts from their British and Canadian allies to citizens who say they have been tortured. If torture undermines a nation's moral legitimacy and proves counterproductive, it also begs the question of what could it mean for the treatment of prisoners captured in future conflicts, especially those who wear US or European military uniforms? Could they be exposed to torture as a direct result of the treatment of detainees in the GWOT?

It has certainly not been lost on the general public that Western journalists and aid workers kidnapped and tortured by the terror group Daesh, also known as Islamic State, have been forced to wear orange Guantanamo-style jump suits while appearing in disturbing propaganda execution videos.

The sickening propaganda video from February 2015 also still haunts many people, as Daesh terrorists put captured Jordanian pilot Moaz al-Kasasbeh in a cage wearing an orange Guantanamo-style boilersuit before setting fire to him. Jordan was one of several Arab allies that had taken part in airstrikes over Syria since September 2014 and against the group in Iraq before then.

Therefore while we can not entirely ignore the moral issues arising from one human being deliberately inflicting pain on another for some form of gain, the main focus of this book will be to explore if torture is a reliable and productive weapon in modern warfare, where often good, solid intelligence can prove to be more potent than the deployment of troops and costly armaments.

The time period for my research encompasses US President George W Bush's ongoing GWOT – declared in response to and shortly after the events of 9/11[8] – up until 2015; other outside factors and influences will also be considered.

For example, the French military experience in Algeria has been revisited by a number of high-profile US military officers,[9] who have drawn parallels from that conflict to the ongoing fight against insurgents in Afghanistan and Iraq. While the regimes in Baghdad and Kabul appeared to collapse relatively quickly, US forces and their allies have spent the following two decades trying to counter and pacify virulent insurgencies in various guises in both countries. There is still ongoing NATO activity in Iraq and Afghanistan and a new terror threat emerging from Daesh in Syria and Iraq, making the need for intelligence gathering both at home and overseas crucial.

It is now widely accepted that some intelligence scrutinised by Western democracies, and the US in particular, was obtained by third-party torture. According to the London-based advocacy group Cage, which began in 2003, most of this intelligence gathering was outsourced[10] and information was extracted under torture from well beyond their legal borders in countries across the Middle East, Africa, the Maghreb, Eastern Europe and Asia.

Cage, using a team of graduate researchers and former GWOT detainees, has argued that there is compelling evidence in the way of documents and memos that some of the intelligence gathered under torture later became more homegrown, according to formerly classified material now released under the US Freedom of Information Act (FOIA).

---

8   Bush, George W: Speech before a Joint Session of Congress, September 20 2001 (Washington DC).

9   "It is not unfair to say that in 2003, most Army officers knew more about the US civil war than they did about counter-insurgency," John Nagl, a retired colonel who served in Iraq, wrote in the foreword to the 2006 *U.S. Army Field Manual 3-24, Counterinsurgency*.

10   Cage website: "Laa Tansa: Never Forget," launched January 10 2012, London. Accessed at   http://www.cageprisoners.com/component/jnews/mailing/view/listid-20/mailingid-75/listype-1/Itemid-999.

But just how reliable was the information given under duress and what, if any, were the direct consequences of evaluating material revealed by terror suspects swept up in the GWOT? To analyse this effectively, a number of opinions were sought, first from those advising the Bush Administration in a legal capacity,[11] using previously classified documents from the National Security Archive (NSA) which were handed over to the American Civil Liberties Union (ACLU) in 2009 following a request using FOIA. Legal opinions were also sought from human rights lawyers and other legal representatives who reflected on the diversity of the argument over the justification for torture.

Most of these views come from primary sources in the US and UK and/or from declassified and redacted documents held in archives in both countries. Thanks to the publication of a number of important autobiographies in 2010 and 2011, opinion formers, decision makers from the White House to Downing Street – from a UK Prime Minister to a US President – have revealed to the wider world their innermost thoughts and decisions taken when they were forced to confront the reality of sanctioning or justifying the use of torture both at home and abroad.

The recollections of those in power all reveal, without exception, how government decisions reached by those at the centre of the GWOT period appeared to forensically examine and internally agonise over professional legal advice offered on the subject of interrogating high-value detainees (HVD) arrested during that incendiary period.

Most of their recollections were published before the December 2014 release of the US Senate Intelligence Committee's 500-page dossier on CIA torture, all of which could prove particularly damning in a future court of law as it would show that a great deal of premeditated, careful analysis and forethought was put into the decision-making procedures used by the Bush Administration.

These key insights contributed to the heated legal arguments submitted to leaders who were forced to seek the opinions of lawmakers. Perhaps it is a cynical observation, but having read the autobiographies of the key figures in the Bush

---

11   These are references to the so-called "Torture Memos," otherwise known as "Standards of Conduct for Interrogation under 18 U.S.C. sections 2340-2340A," "Interrogation of al Qaeda" and an untitled letter from legal advisers, including then US Attorney General, Alberto Gonzales; the Assistant Attorney General, Jay Bybee; and a former official in the US States Department of Justice, John Choon Yoo, from January 2002 through to 2009. All are freely available from the ACLU website, accessed at http://www.aclu.org/ and are also reproduced in Greenburg, Karen J, Dratel, Joshua L: The Torture Papers: The Road to Abu Ghraib, Cambridge University Press, 2005.

Administration, one has to ask if the White House lawyers and legal advisers were used as a defensive shield should the President and his inner circle be accused in later years of endorsing practices deemed illegal under domestic and international law.

Significantly, the Malaysia War Crimes Tribunal[12] convened in Kuala Lumpur for a week from 7 May 2012 ruled that politicians were judged to be equally responsible and held to account as those advising them on a legal basis.

While potential critics of the tribunal, including Param Cumaraswamy, former UN Special Rapporteur on the Independence of Judges and Lawyers,[13] may try to dismiss the initiative as nothing more than a publicity stunt supported by Asia's longest-serving Prime Minister,[14] Tun Mahathir Mohamad, it would be reckless to ignore the outcomes of its trials.

As I sat through the tribunal listening to the evidence, the former PM told me that he launched the project in 2007 as an alternative to the International Criminal Court (ICC)[15] because he had: *"no faith or trust in the ICC and therefore I created a new body to hear war crimes which would use the same legal protocols as the Nuremberg Trials."*

Despite being steeped in controversy the tribunal went on to find Bush, his Vice President Richard "Dick" Cheney, Defense Secretary Donald Rumsfeld and their legal advisers Alberto Gonzales, David Addington, William Haynes, Jay Bybee and John Yoo guilty in absentia of "torture and cruel, inhumane and degrading treatment."

---

12   A Kuala Lumpur-based initiative established in 2007 by former Prime Minister Mahathir Mohamad to investigate alleged war crimes as an alternative to the ICC in The Hague.

13   In a letter he wrote in Malaysiakini, Cumaraswamy said there was no legal basis for the tribunal, which would become a "circus." Malaysiakini is the country's most widely read news website, accessed at http://www.malaysiakini.com/letters/6331.

14   He was the fourth PM of Malaysia in the 22 years from 1981 to 2003. For more, read: *A Doctor in the House ... The Memoirs of Tun Dr Mahathir Mohamad*, MPA Publishing, Malaysia, 2011.

15   Launched on July 1 2002; a permanent tribunal to prosecute individuals for war crimes, including genocide and crimes against humanity. Sudan, Israel and America have all withdrawn from the ICC.

As a counterbalance to the clinical and calculated reasonings of various members of the judiciary and politicians, the personal views from recipients of torture, including a number of ex-Guantanamo (GTMO) detainees[16] swept up in the GWOT, also were sought. Several members of the Libyan Islamic Fighting Group (LIFG) also agreed to give their personal accounts of torture at the hands of the former Western ally, the late Colonel Gadaffi.[17]

It is important to note that none of those interviewed specifically for this book has ever been convicted of, charged with or tried for terror-related offences.[18] As mentioned previously, all of the ex-GTMO detainees who are British residents or citizens have received compensation running into hundreds of thousands of pounds from the UK Government which has also offered to conduct an inquiry into their cases.[19] Lawyers for some of the LIFG men interviewed are currently in compensatory negotiations with the UK Government.[20]

Striking the right balance in the face of the passionate and emotional arguments presented by human rights groups, who described Guantanamo Bay as "a gulag of our time,"[21] proved to be challenging as defenders of torture resorted to a less inflammatory or excitable tone when recounting the legal and moral case for endorsing its use.

For instance, US Vice President Cheney rejected the "gulag" adjectives invoked by Guantanamo, preferring instead to use more mundane and less provocative language. He said it was, indeed, a *"model facility—safe, secure, and humane. It likely provides a standard of care higher than many prisons in European countries where the criticism of Guantanamo has been loudest."*[22]

---

16 The Guantanamo Bay prisons or holding facilities opened at the US Naval Base in Cuba in January 2002 under the operation of the Joint Task Force Guantanamo (JTF-GTMO).

17 For more on Gadaffi, see: Gadaffi, Muammar: *My Vision*, John Blake Publishing, London, 2005; and Kawczynski, Daniel: *Seeking Gadaffi*, Dialogue, Colorado, 2011.ff

18 Ex-detainees who have agreed to co-operate and talk about their personal experiences for the purposes of the research include British citizens and residents *Moazzam Begg, Tarek Derghoul, Feroz Abbassi* and several ex-LIFG members, including *Abdul Hakim Belhadj, Mohamed Rebaii and Sami al Saadi.*

19 Norton-Taylor, Richard: "Guantanamo: Security Services Must Be Protected, Says Ken Clarke." *The Guardian*, p. 5, November 17 2010.

20 Norton-Taylor, Richard: "Straw, MI6 and Libyan Renditions: An Issue that Will Not Go Away." *The Guardian*, p. 5, April 18 2012.

21 Norton-Taylor, Richard: "Guantanamo Is Gulag of our Time, Says Amnesty." *The Guardian*, May 26 2005.

22 Cheney, Dick: *In My Time*, New York, Threshold, August 2011, p. 35.

As a counterbalance, in recently published autobiographies,[23, 24, 25] senior members of the Bush Administration, including the US President[26] himself, relate their justification for the use of torture during the GWOT as well as the backdrop that influenced their motivations and fears. The autobiography of the former British Prime Minister Tony Blair[27] is also used as a source to reflect the decision making taken from the other side of the Atlantic with reference to the GWOT.

It is now known and accepted by a former top aide[28] that some of the information used by US Secretary of State Colin Powell at the United Nations on February 5 2003 to push the case for a war in Iraq was supplied as a result of torture carried out on terror suspect Ibn Sheikh al-Libi who died in a Libyan prison in May 2009.[29] The importance of the al-Libi confession can not be understated and the emergence of new material about what happened to this man after his torture in Cairo is revealed for the first time in these pages.

An exclusive interview given and recorded on video by Sheikh Mohamed Bosidra[30] in Benghazi in March 2011 for my investigations into torture reveals more information about the actual methods performed on al-Libi. This information is largely corroborated by the authors of two books, and they will be further sourced and verified,[31] but Bosidra's account is convincing and has not been widely publicized before.

---

23   Cheney: *In My Time.*

24   Rice, Condoleezza: *No Higher Honour,* Simon & Schuster UK Ltd., 2011

25   Rumsfeld, Donald: *Known and Unknown, A Memoir.* New York, Penguin Group, 2011

26   Bush, George W: *Decision Points,* London, Virgin Books, 2010.

27   Blair, Tony: *A Journey,* London, Arrow Books, 2010.

28   Col. Lawrence Wilkerson, a longtime adviser to Colin Powell who served as his chief of staff from 2002 through 2005 said: "I look back on it, and I still say it was the lowest point in my life," during a CNN interview into the presentation made before the UN on February 5 2003. The interview was used for the CNN presents documentary "Dead Wrong – Inside an Intelligence Meltdown" in August 2005.

29   A Libyan terror suspect, born Ali Mohamed al-Fakheri (1963–10 May 2009), was captured and interrogated by the American and Egyptian forces. Information he gave under torture by Egyptian authorities was cited by the George W Bush Administration in the months preceding the 2003 invasion of Iraq as evidence of a connection between Saddam Hussein and al-Qaeda.

30   Sheikh Mohamed Bosidra was in a cell adjacent to al-Libi in Abu Salim prison and recounts what happened to the Libyan after he was arrested in Pakistan and renditioned to the US Airbase in Bagram, Afghanistan.

31   Risen, James: *State of War. The Secret History of the CIA and the Bush Administration,* 2006; and Mayer, Jane: *The Dark Side: The Inside Story of How the War on Terror Turned into a War on American Ideals.* Garden City NY: Doubleday, 2008, p. 105.

It is essential not to underestimate the central role played by al-Libi's torture in the GWOT as his confession under duress was used to start the war in Iraq. It was only some months after the conflict had begun that it emerged the confession, extracted by inflicting extreme pain on him, turned out to be completely fabricated. The head of Human Rights Watch (HRW), based in Washington, stated that al-Libi was "Exhibit A" in hearings on the relationship between pre-Iraq War false intelligence and torture.[32]

Not only did the torture of al-Libi in Cairo produce false information that was used in Colin Powell's powerful UN speech to argue for the invasion of Iraq, but it also had a domino effect which resulted in the arrests of nine Algerian men living in the UK[33] who were accused of manufacturing the poison Ricin.[34] It could also be argued that the sensational media headlines caused unnecessary fear and panic among Londoners that they were the original targets of the so-called Ricin Gang.

It was some three years later that it emerged the Algerian arrests were linked to the faulty intelligence gathered during the Cairo torture of al-Libi, as published in a book[35] co-written by Lawrence Archer. Archer was a juror in the case of the so-called Ricin Plot which he concludes was exposed as "pure invention" in April 2005 after the six-month trial.[36]

By the time al-Libi's false confession was discredited, the war in Iraq was well underway with the civilian death toll there running into six figures.

While the evidence given by Colin Powell before the UN and the outcome of the Ricin trial throws doubt on the reliability of using intelligence gathered by torture, a series of academics, politicians and students of academia on both sides of the Atlantic have sprung to its defence by citing the so-called Ticking Bomb scenario.[37]

---

32   Finn, Peter: "Detainee Who Gave False Iraq Data Dies in Libya." *Washington* Post, May 12 2009.

33   *The Daily Mirror* newspaper showed a skull and crossbones against a map of Britain on its Wednesday front page under the headline "It's here." The Sun, Britain's biggest circulation daily, said the discovery revealed a "factory of death." London, January 8 2003.

34   Ricin is produced from the castor oil plant Ricinus communis and is highly toxic. A dose as small as a few grains of salt can kill an adult.

35   Archer, Lawrence and Bawdon, Fiona: *Ricin! The Inside Story of the Terror Plot that Never Was.* London, Pluto Press, 2010.

36   Campbell, Duncan: "The Ricin Ring that Never Was." *The Guardian*, World News, April 14 2005.

37   Lartéguy, Jean: *Les Centurions* is a 1960s novel in which the Ticking Bomb scenario was introduced into the plot, written around the brutal French occupation of Algeria. In 1966, The Centurions was adapted into a motion picture, "Lost Command," starring Anthony Quinn.

It is this scenario that will be looked at exhaustively here as it is the key argument used by the pro-torture lobby. Harvard University law professor Alan Dershowitz famously clashed on American TV with Ken Roth, the executive director of HRW, over the use of torture when he advocated that it should be done as a "last resort" but openly and with accountability.[38]

One of the most comprehensive arguments endorsing torture was put forward by Western Michigan University student Fritz Allhoff,[39] who authored a book and article[40, 41] on the much-publicised Ticking Bomb scenario.

In addition the liberal newspaper The Independent ran a robust opinion piece by Bruce Anderson, one of its more right-wing columnists and political journalists, advocating the use of torture[42] while the late Christopher Hitchens, who was anti-torture, underwent waterboarding[43] to make a personal judgement on whether he considered waterboarding a method of torture or not.[44]

Meanwhile in Australia, professor of law Mirko Bagaric and law lecturer Julie Clarke challenged those who say that even to debate the issue of torture is morally reprehensible, and published a book[45] presenting a strong case for its use. The contents of all of these books and articles are used here to investigate clinically, and without emotion, the arguments used to promote the use of torture and the end benefits of such practices in relation to the GWOT.

---

38   CNN.com/Law Center: Interview conducted by Wolf Blitzer.

39   Associate Professor in the Department of Philosophy at Western Michigan University and a Senior Research Fellow at The Australian National University's Centre for Applied Philosophy and Public Ethics. Accessed at http://www.allhoff.org/.

40   Fritz Allhoff says on his website http://www.allhoff.org/research/ that his primary research interests are in ethical theory, applied ethics and philosophy of biology.

41   Allhoff, Fritz: *Terrorism, Ticking Time-Bombs, and Torture.* University of Chicago Press, 2012

42   Anderson, Bruce: "We Not Only Have a Right to Use Torture. We Have a Duty." *The Independent*, London, February 15 2010.

43   The process of waterboarding involves immobilising the victim while pouring water on a cloth covering his/her face to create the sensation of drowning. It can cause extreme pain; dry drowning; damage to lungs; brain damage from oxygen deprivation; other physical injuries, including broken bones due to struggling against restraints; lasting psychological damage and death.

44   Hitchens, Christopher: "Believe Me, It's Torture." *Vanity Fair*, New York, August 2008.

45   Bagaric, Mirko and Clarke, Julie: Torture. *When the Unthinkable Is Morally Permissible.* Albany NY, State University of New York Press, 2007.

The thrust of their arguments is that it is morally preferable to inflict pain to break someone's will than allow innocents to be murdered. Because of "national security" it may be difficult to come up with exact instances in which this has happened, although several prominent politicians and intelligence chiefs have stated it to be the case without citing specific examples.

This absence exposes the weakness of the "pro-torture lobby" argument because very few of its defenders can come up with specific examples in which the torture of an individual has prevented a much bigger crime. Alan Dershowitz mooted the idea of introducing torture warrants, using carefully constructed arguments which critics said would lead to the legalising of torture.

However, so far, he has failed to name a single event in any of his books or papers in which inflicting pain on individuals has led to the prevention of a crime.[46] He does, however, cite the interrogation of the mother of Abu Nidal[47] that in turn broke down the ruthless Palestinian terrorist leader in the 1980s as evidence of the successful use of torture. Nevertheless, it is worth noting that Nidal's mother was a third-party innocent, a fact which contradicts previous arguments submitted by Dershowitz that controlled torture should be carried out only on terror suspects.

In the context of Nidal's mother he singles Jordan out as a state prepared to carry out torture with a degree of success. In one article[48] he wrote:

> *"Jordan has perfected the art of torture and uses it routinely against dissidents, suspected terrorists and perceived opponents of the monarchy. I'm talking about real torture here, not the kind of rough interrogation occasionally employed by the US and Israel. Jordan even threatens to torture and tortures the entirely innocent relatives of suspected terrorists, as it did with Abu Nidal's mother."*

---

46   Brecher, Bob: *Torture and the Ticking Bomb.* Blackwell Publishing, 2007, p. 25.

47   Abu Nidal, real name Sabri Khalil al-Banna. He was the founder of Fatah –The Revolutionary Council, a militant Palestinian group known in the Western media as the Abu Nidal Organization (ANO). At the height of his power in the 1970s and 1980s Abu Nidal was widely regarded as the most ruthless of the Palestinian political leaders.

48   Professor Alan Morton Dershowitz, an American lawyer, jurist and political commentator. Newsweek described him as "the nation's most peripatetic civil liberties lawyer and one of its most distinguished defenders of individual rights." Dershowitz, Alan M: "The Case Against Jordan." *Jerusalem Post*, October 9 2003, reproduced in several online publications, including Frontpagemag.com, accessed at http://archive.frontpagemag.com/readArticle.aspx?ARTID=15992.

Long before the waterboarding debate went public, former CIA agent John Kiriakou admitted that he felt the practice was torture but also revealed in his own book[49] that it probably did work on a number of terror suspects and produced positive results that may have prevented a series of specific attacks.

Until now Kiriakou is the only CIA official who participated in the torture program who has been punished after going public in 2007 about the interrogation tactics used by the agency. After he was sent to prison, he wrote: *"In truth, this is my punishment for blowing the whistle on the CIA's illegal torture program and for telling the public that torture was official US government policy."*

The evidence and conclusions he gives in his book support the pro-torture lobby's claim that torture is a necessary evil which works and saves lives. It was additionally backed by a now famous interview he later gave on US television when he claimed that a terror suspect had "cracked" 35 seconds into being waterboarded.[50] It has now emerged that his knowledge of the CIA waterboarding program and the torture of Abu Zubaydah in particular was second hand, but at the time, he offered reluctant support for the pro-torture lobby. However, he later retracted his beliefs after discovering that he had been lied to about its efficacy.

Waterboarding has now become almost synonymous with the name of Khalid Sheikh Mohammed, known in the intelligence community as KSM. His particular treatment and the source of intelligence gathered as a result will be scrutinised in particular because of all the detainees in the GWOT, KSM is probably the most notorious in the public's mind.

Although the period under scrutiny covers the GWOT years, it would be imprudent to ignore a wealth of documents recently declassified from the UK National Archives which look at the interrogation methods developed by the commandant of a previously little known top-secret detention facility[51] in London during World War II.

---

49   Kiriakou, John: *The Reluctant Spy: My Secret Life in the CIA's War on Terror.* New York, Bantam Books, 2009.

50   Kiriakou, a 15-year veteran of the agency's intelligence analysis and operations directorates, sparked a national debate in the US over torture in December 2007 when he told ABC's Brian Ross and Richard Esposito that senior al-Qaeda commando Abu Zubaydah became confessional after one waterboarding. For more information on his retraction, see http://foreignpolicy.com/2010/01/26/cia-man-retracts-claim-on-waterboarding/.

51   Latchmere House in West London was MI5's holding centre for captured enemy agents.

The manuscript,[52] written as the official record of MI5's operations at Camp 020, will be referred to in great detail to contrast and compare interrogation techniques used by the intelligence services in the UK between 1940 and 1945 and US intelligence since 9/11.

Until its declassification in 1999 very few outside of intelligence circles knew anything about the history and role of the rambling, three-storey Latchmere House in Surrey, which was first briefly mentioned by the late historian and espionage author Ladislas Farago in a couple of paragraphs of his book "The Game of the Foxes",[53] where he wrote:

> *"When MI5 needed a detention center off the beaten path, it borrowed the old mental institution, so well hidden from curious eyes and easy to guard. The hush-hush place was tolerated, or ignored by the good people of Ham. No questions were asked, not even when it was rumored in the village that Rudolf Hess had arrived at the House."*

In conclusion, it is worth noting that I personally wrestled with the question of torture after being arrested and detained by Afghanistan's ruling Taliban regime shortly after the events of 9/11.[54] I was still being held in a prison cell on the night the US-led war began on October 7 2001.

The issue of torture became very real issue for me as I agonized over how I would react in the event of being tortured. I recounted this in a book on my experiences[55] and made a conscious decision at the time to sign anything that was put before me, regardless of how outrageous, to prevent at any cost being tortured by the Taliban.

Having first established the definition of torture, the moral and legal arguments for and against its use, personal accounts from victims of torture, its short-term and long-term consequences, as well as its effectiveness in intelligence gathering, public perceptions and international opinion, the conclusion of this work will endeavour to answer the question of its efficacy in a definitive way.

---

52   Lt Col Robin Stephens: *A Digest of Ham.* Declassified in September 1999.
53   Farago, Ladislas: *The Game of the Foxes.* New York, David McKay Company, 1971, p. 329.
54   While serving as Sunday Express chief reporter, I was arrested by the Taliban on September 28 2001. Suspected of spying, I was apprehended near Jalalabad without a passport and visa and held for 11 days before being released on humanitarian grounds.
55   Ridley, Yvonne: *In the Hands of the Taliban*, London, Robson Books, 2001.

The only way of reaching a satisfactory conclusion is to suspend legal and moral judgements to avoid clouding the real thrust of this book. In short: Does Torture Work? By answering this question in full and weighing up the side effects of its legacy, we will then be able to establish if torture is an effective weapon of modern warfare which should be considered part of the arsenal of a military machine in the 21st century, alongside smart bombs and drones.

The methods and results will be evaluated in the same way as an expert would test a gun to see if it is a worthy weapon in a modern army. For instance, what use is a gun if it produces no bullets or misfires more often than not?

2
Defining Torture

To fully comprehend the question of whether torture works or not it is essential to understand exactly what torture is beyond the rather broad and simple definitions given in dictionaries, such as the online Oxford Dictionaries, which simply describe it as being:

"The action or practice of inflicting severe pain on someone as a punishment or in order to force them to do or say something."[1]

The word itself originates from the classical Latin noun "tortūra" which, loosely translated, means a twisting effect; however, it is a word in daily usage which has been used and misused in many contradictory ways on an almost casual basis by people who really give little thought to what it actually means.

This casual use is illustrated almost perfectly by celebrities, from Russian chess player Garry Kasparov, who described his game as "mental torture," to the actor Juliet Stevenson, who once said: "I sometimes think that theatre is torture."

Various establishments and groups from the United Nations to non-governmental organisations (NGOs) have invested a great deal of thought about what the word really does mean, however, and have developed their own interpretation and definition of what constitutes torture – whether inflicted by a state, individuals or groups.

In 1973 the human rights organisation Amnesty International [2] (AI) adopted a very simple, broad definition describing torture as follows:

---

1   Oxford Dictionaries Online, online reference for torture. Accessed at http://oxforddictionaries. com/definition/torture.

2   Amnesty International was founded in 1961 as a human rights organization; it now has in excess of 3 million members globally.

"The systematic and deliberate infliction of acute pain by one person on another, or on a third person, in order to accomplish the purpose of the former against the will of the latter."[3]

By 1977 AI was rewarded for its efforts and expertise in this field by being presented with the Nobel Peace Prize for its campaign against torture.[4] During the same decade a group of doctors gathered at the 29th General Assembly of the World Medical Association (WMA) [5] where another, slightly more elaborate definition was drawn up as follows:

"For the purpose of this Declaration, torture is defined as the deliberate, systematic or wanton infliction of physical or mental suffering by one or more persons acting alone or on the orders of any authority, to force another person to yield information, to make a confession, or for any other reason."[6]

By the 1980s the issue of torture appeared to emerge as a growing concern on the international stage, and so the United Nations Convention Against Torture (UNCAT) was established on December 10 1984 at the 39th session of the General Assembly of the United Nations in New York. The majority of member states signed the Treaty, with a number of countries adding individual declarations and reservations upon ratification in the years that followed.[7] The aim at its inception was to prevent torture around the world, including the outlawing of torture within country borders as well as the banning of transporting of individuals to a country where there is reason to believe they would be submitted to torture.

From the perspective of this chapter the most significant section of UNCAT is contained within Part 1, in which the UN outlines its definition of torture. It reads as follows:

---

3   Amnesty International: *Torture in the Eighties*. USA Edition. Amnesty International Publication, 1973.

4   The Nobel Peace Prize is regarded by some as one of the most prestigious prizes in the world.

5   An international and independent confederation formally established on September 18 1947 that by 2011 had incorporated 97 National Medical Associations involving more than 10 million physicians.

6   The WMA Declaration of Tokyo (October 1975), Section 5.

7   United Nations, Treaty Series, 1465, p. 85.

"Any act by which severe pain or suffering, whether physical or mental, is intentionally inflicted on a person for such purposes as obtaining from him or a third person, information or a confession, punishing him for an act he or a third person has committed or is suspected of having committed, or intimidating or coercing him or a third person, or for any reason based on discrimination of any kind, when such pain or suffering is inflicted by or at the instigation of or with the consent or acquiescence of a public official or other person acting in an official capacity. It does not include pain or suffering arising only from, inherent in or incidental to lawful sanctions."[8]

Two years later, in 1986, the World Health Organisation (WHO)[9] established a working group and, while drawing up its own definition of torture, introduced the concept of organised violence. The definition reads as follows:

"The inter-human infliction of significant, avoidable pain and suffering by an organised group according to a declared or implied strategy and/or system of ideas and attitudes. It comprises any violent action that is unacceptable by general human standards, and relates to the victims' feelings. Organized violence includes 'torture, cruel, inhuman or degrading treatment or punishment' as in Article 5 of the United Nations Universal Declaration of Human Rights (1984). Imprisonment without trial, mock executions, hostage-taking, or any other form of violent deprivation of liberty, also fall under the heading of organised violence."[10]

Despite the definitions clearly outlined by such august bodies as the UN, human rights groups and medical and health organisations, there are those who have attempted to redefine torture, some with the aim of justifying the actions of interrogation teams' training following the events of 9/11.[11] Lawyers and politicians appeared to create a new set of rules and would later either be supported or held to rigorous account by their colleagues as well as academics and journalists as their interpretations were defined.

All of the above definitions would be pored over forensically from 2002 onwards and used as a base by lawyers from the Bush Administration before they reached any conclusions about new proposed methods of interrogation.

---

8   UN Convention Against Torture, Article 1.1 United Nations, December 10 1984.

9   The WHO was set up on April 7 1948 as a specialised agency of the UN concerned about public health internationally.

10   A report on a WHO meeting: "The Health Hazards of Organised Violence." Veldhoven, April 22–25 1986.

11   The September 11 2001 attacks in which 19 airline hijackers organised four co-ordinated attacks upon the USA in which nearly 3,000 civilians died.

It was several years after the events of September 11 2001 that the subject of torture was propelled into the public arena to become one of the most hotly debated and contested issues of the same decade that saw the launch of the GWOT.

Along with the GWOT came a new vocabulary, using rather covert and secretive terms at first; now, however, phrases like extraordinary rendition, ghost detainees, black sites, waterboarding and enhanced interrogation are quite familiar. Each of these will be explained in more detail in the forthcoming pages.

In his autobiography[12] US President George W Bush gives an insight into the thought processes and decisions taken over allowing intelligence agencies to perform "enhanced interrogation" on certain high-profile terror suspects[13] using methods such as waterboarding, which some viewed as crossing a line based on the above definitions of torture.[14]

One of the major obstacles in the treatment and interrogation of terror suspects encountered by the Bush Administration were the Geneva Conventions (GC),[15] of which the US was one of the signers. As a signatory, America had agreed on a specific code of conduct over the treatment of prisoners of war (POWs). However there were those in the Bush Administration who argued that terrorists were not eligible to POW status and thus fell out of the GC remit; the US Vice President was the first to lead the charge, according to Washington Post journalist Barton Gellman who wrote as follows:[16]

> *"The next day, November 14, 2001, Cheney took another bold step. He told the U.S. Chamber of Commerce that a terrorist does not 'deserve to be treated as a prisoner of war.' The President had not yet made that decision. Ten weeks passed, and his advisers fought a fierce internal brawl, before Bush ratified the policy that Cheney declared: The Geneva Conventions would not apply to al Qaida or Taliban fighters."*

Could it be that Cheney was attempting to create a legal cocktail from the two main branches of international humanitarian law – the law of The Hague and the law of Geneva? While the former sets out the methods of warfare and governs the

---

12   Bush, *Decision Points*, p. 168–171.

13   Abu Zubaydah, Ramzi bin Al Shibh, KSM.

14   Levinson, Stanford: *Torture, A Collection*. Oxford University Press, 2004.

15   The Geneva Conventions are a series of treaties on the treatment of civilians, prisoners of war and soldiers who are in other ways rendered incapable of fighting.

16   Gellman, Barton: *Angler: The Cheney Vice Presidency*. New York, Penguin Group, 2008.

actual conduct of hostilities or rules of war, the latter is codified within a series of conventions set up in 1949 to address the concerns and protections of civilians, the wounded and POWs.

Of the four Geneva Conventions signed by the US, Conventions I and III specifically refer to torture as being a forbidden practice. All four are outlined below and make no special mention to the status or rights of terrorists:

Convention I:[17] *This convention protects wounded and infirm soldiers and medical personnel against attack, execution without judgment, torture and assault upon personal dignity (Article 3). It also grants them the right to proper medical treatment and care.*

Convention II:[18] *This agreement extends the protections mentioned in the first convention to shipwrecked soldiers and other naval forces, including special protections afforded to hospital ships.*

Convention III:[19] *One of the treaties created during the 1949 convention, it defines a prisoner of war and accords prisoners of war proper and humane treatment as specified by the first convention. Specifically, it requires POWs to give only their name, rank and serial number to a captor. Nations party to the convention may not use torture to extract information from POWs.*

Convention IV:[20] *Under this convention, civilians are afforded the protections from inhumane treatment and attack afforded in the first convention to sick and wounded*

---

17   This Convention represents the fourth updated version of the Geneva Convention on the wounded and sick, following those adopted in 1864, 1906 and 1929. It contains 64 articles.

18   This Convention replaced the Hague Convention of 1907 for the Adaptation to Maritime Warfare of the Principles of the Geneva Convention. It has 63 articles specifically applicable to war at sea.

19   This Convention replaced the Prisoners of War Convention of 1929. It contains 143 articles, whereas the 1929 Convention had only 97. The categories of persons entitled to POW status are broadened in accordance with Conventions I and II. The conditions and places of captivity are more precisely defined, particularly with regard to the labour of prisoners of war, their financial resources, the relief they receive and the judicial proceedings instituted against them. The Convention establishes the principle that prisoners of war shall be released and repatriated without delay after the cessation of active hostilities. It has five annexes containing various model regulations and identity and other cards.

20   The GCs were adopted before 1949 and concerned combatants only. This convention is composed of 159 articles and contains a short section concerning the general protection of populations against certain consequences of war.

soldiers. Furthermore, additional regulations regarding the treatment of civilians are introduced. Specifically, it prohibits attacks on civilian hospitals, medical transports, etc. It also specifies the right of internees and those who commit acts of sabotage. Finally, it discusses how occupiers are to treat an occupied populace.

While the US ratified the four conventions, it has yet to ratify the additional protocols that followed. The first two protocols were adopted in 1977. They strengthen the protection of victims of international (Protocol I) and non-international (Protocol II) armed conflicts and place limits on the way wars are fought. In 2005, a third additional protocol was adopted, creating an additional emblem, the Red Crystal, which has the same international status as the Red Cross and Red Crescent emblems. The protocols are outlined below:

Protocol I: In this additional protocol to the Geneva Conventions, the signing nations agreed to further restrictions on the treatment of "protected persons" according to the original conventions. Furthermore, clarification of the terms used in the conventions was introduced. Finally, new rules regarding the treatment of the deceased, cultural artifacts and dangerous targets (such as dams and nuclear installations) were produced.

Protocol II: In this protocol, the fundamentals of "humane treatment" were further clarified. Additionally, the rights of interned persons were specifically enumerated, providing protections for those charged with crimes during wartime. It also identified new protections and rights of civilian populations.

Protocol III: Since the 19th century, the Red Cross and Red Crescent emblems have been used as universal symbols of assistance for armed conflict victims. The new emblem introduced in this protocol is the Red Crystal — Protocol III was drawn up in such a way as to prevent the emergence of additional emblems in the future.

The 1949 conventions and their additional protocols are at the core of international humanitarian law[21] and are designed specifically to protect people who are taken prisoner in wars as well as those deemed not to be taking part in conflicts, such as civilians, health and aid workers, and the wounded and sick who might also fall into the prisoner category.

---

21   This is the body of international law that regulates the conduct of armed conflict and seeks to limit its effects.

While the definitions of torture outlined in this chapter and referenced in the GCs were generally accepted by various key members of the Bush Administration, including the US President himself, the debates continued as to whether members of the terrorist group al-Qaeda,[22] the Taliban[23] and other terror suspects failed to qualify as POWs and thus should not be accorded rights under the GCs. They were collectively termed as "unlawful enemy combatants" because they did not belong to a conventional army, wear uniforms or abide by the rules of engagement as set out in the conventions, including the targeting of innocent civilians.

However, the redefining of enemy combatants triggered fears in some quarters that if the Bush Administration was prepared to create new terms of reference it might also redefine torture and/or the methods of interrogation deployed to extract human intelligence.

It could be argued that this move was unusual but not new. During World War II the domestic intelligence service MI5 had established a secure facility called Camp 020, which held civilian prisoners for intelligence purposes outside of the GC. This facility will be explored in more detail later in this book because, according to Colonel Stephens' notes, the ethos of 020 was based on non-violent interrogations.

However, nine days following the aftermath of 9/11, Congress passed a resolution[24] invoking the already existing War Powers resolution[25] set out below:

> *"That the President is authorized to use all necessary and appropriate force against those nations, organizations, or persons he determines planned, authorized, committed, or aided the terrorist attacks that occurred on September 11, 2001, or harbored such organizations or persons, in order to prevent any future acts of international terrorism against the United States by such nations, organizations, or persons."*

---

22   A global broad-based Islamic group founded by Osama bin Laden.

23   The Taliban ruled large parts of Afghanistan from 1996 until 2001, when they were overthrown by Operation Enduring Freedom.

24   The Authorization for Use of Military Force (AUMF) was passed on September 18 2001.

25   This resolution is a federal law that allows a US President to send the US military into action abroad only by authorisation of Congress or in case of "a national emergency created by attack upon the United States, its territories or possessions, or its armed forces."

Using the authorisation granted to him by Congress,[26] nearly two months later President Bush issued this Presidential Military Order:

> *"Detention, Treatment, and Trial of Certain Non-Citizens in the War Against Terrorism" which allowed "individuals ... to be detained, and, when tried, to be tried for violations of the laws of war and other applicable laws by military tribunals" where "... such individuals are a member of the organization known as al Qa'ida ... or ... conspired or committed acts of international terrorism ... or have as their aim to cause injury to or adverse effects on the United States, its citizens, national security, foreign policy, or economy."*

Choosing to refer to detainees as "illegal enemy combatants," the order failed to elaborate or specify the length of time terror suspects could be detained, nor did the order reveal any details of methods of interrogation. However, as if to pre-empt his critics, the US President added the final line: *"The order also specifies that the detainees are to be treated humanely."*

In two written notes to President Bush, White House Counsel Alberto R Gonzales[27] advised him that he did not have to comply with the GCs in handling detainees in the GWOT. This advice applied not only to members of al-Qaeda but the entire Taliban because, he argued, Afghanistan was a "failed state."[28]

Despite opposition from the US State Department,[29] which warned Gonzales against ignoring the GCs, the Bush Administration began holding individuals at the Guantanamo Bay US Naval Base in Cuba beginning in January 2002. The research in the later chapters of this book investigates more closely the legal advice given to President Bush and his successor, President Barack Obama, and their responses.

Returning to the focus on the definition of torture, it appears that some elements of the Bush Administration wanted to introduce new and tougher methods of

---

26   President George W Bush's Military Order on November 13 2001: "Detention, Treatment, and Trial of Certain Non-Citizens in the War Against Terrorism."

27   Alberto R Gonzales at various times served as both White House Counsel and Attorney General of the United States.

28   Contained in a declassified memorandum on January 18 2002 from Gonzales to the US President and repeated in a second draft memorandum on January 25 2002; now part of a public archive known as *The Torture Papers*.

29   Referenced in a declassified memorandum from Colin Powell, Secretary of State in response to the Gonzales draft memorandum of January 25 2002.

interrogation within the ranks of the CIA,[30] when it emerged that gathering intelligence from some enemy combatants was proving more challenging than previously anticipated.

In his own words, CIA Agent John Kiriakou wrote as follows:

> *"After 9/11 we were in a different war ... and there was no modus operandi in place for the treatment of captured bad guys ... That didn't mean we were operating with no guidance at all. When I got to Pakistan in late January 2002, and we started to interrogate people, our marching orders were fairly straightforward: We knew that we weren't allowed to hit anyone, to threaten anyone, to torture ... What became clear fairly soon was that it would be very difficult to get useful information from this new breed of enemy ... for whom death meant religious martyrdom and a one-way ticket to paradise."[31]*

Kiriakou believes the turning point in the redefining of interrogation, which involved the need for "harsher treatment," was brought about by the capture on March 8 2002 in Faisalabad, Pakistan of a senior al-Qaeda operative known as Abu Zubaydah.

Zubaydah had been shot three times and required round-the-clock medical attention to save his life but, as he recovered, Kiriakou revealed in his book that the captive was *"belligerent at the beginning and wouldn't co-operate a bit. Eventually, that would change, after we handed him off to the group that flew him from Pakistan to another overseas location."*

It is clear that at this stage Zubaydah was regarded as a hugely prized asset and taken to a black site[32] by CIA agents who had been trained in "enhanced techniques" for interrogation of high-value terror suspects.

The removal of Zubaydah presented Kiriakou with an agonising dilemma if he wanted to remain in a lead role during the interrogation. He wrote as follows:

---

30   Kiriakou: *Reluctant Spy*, p. 130.
31   Kiriakou: *Reluctant Spy*, p. 129.
32   In military terminology, such sites are at locations where an unacknowledged black project is being conducted.

"We had some inkling of what these enhanced techniques entailed, enough to impel me to seek counsel from a top CIA officer I respected enormously. He suggested to me that these methods might well cross a dangerous moral and legal line, and I declined to be trained in them."[33]

Until that point, it was clear that Kiriakou, who had led the CIA operation that tracked down the Saudi-born Zubaydah, would have been expected to continue playing a key role in the interrogation of the detainee. The fact that he reluctantly stood aside, refusing to be trained in "enhanced interrogation" techniques (EITs), suggests he felt such procedures were crossing a legal line.

It was not until 2008 when the Justice Department, responding to a court order, released a report by the CIA inspector general that EITs were revealed to have bordered on torture. As a result, US Attorney General (AG) Eric Holder[34] ordered a preliminary inquiry to see if the behaviour of the CIA interrogators and their contractors warranted a full criminal investigation.

The following year, Holder released 16 pages of declassified narratives[35] describing the Department of Justice legal counsel's opinions on the CIA's detention and interrogation programmes to Senator John Davison "Jay" Rockefeller.[36]

There were strong suspicions that the interrogations teams had redefined torture in 2002; several years later, stories began to emerge in the US media. One of the most significant was a Washington Post[37] story that revealed how in September 2002 four members of Congress had received secret briefings on the harsh techniques devised for overseas detention sites where top al-Qaeda operatives were being held.[38]

The article in the Washington Post revealed the following:

---

33   Kiriakou: *Reluctant Spy*, p. 133.

34   Eric Holder served as AG under President Barack Obama from 2009 to 2015.

35   Holder letter and declassified US intelligence documents to Rockefeller, accessed at http://intelligence.senate.gov/pdfs/olcopinion.pdf.

36   Jay Rockefeller IV is a Democrat who sat on the US Senate Select Committee on Intelligence.

37   *The Washington Post* is the largest and most influential daily newspaper in Washington, DC.

38   Warrick, Joby and Eggen, Dan: "Hill Briefed on Waterboarding in 2002." *Washington Post*, front page Sunday, December 9, 2007.

"Among the techniques described, said two officials present, was waterboarding, a practice that years later would be condemned as torture by Democrats and some Republicans on Capitol Hill. But on that day, no objections were raised. Instead, at least two lawmakers in the room asked the CIA to push harder, two U.S. officials said."

Politicians from all sides joined in the debate over the waterboarding issue, asking if it fell within the definitions of torture. AG nominee Michael B. Mukasey[39] refused to classify the practice as torture; his reluctance even threatened to derail his hearing for the post of AG[40] while being questioned by the Senate Judiciary Committee (SJC)[41] for the job. During the panel interview, all ten Democratic representatives expressed frustration at his "unwillingness to state waterboarding is illegal." [42]

A Republican politician who had no doubt of the status of waterboarding was US Senator John McCain who was himself a one-time victim of torture when he was held as a POW in Vietnam.[43] In a telephone interview[44] with a New York Times journalist, he stated: *"All I can say is that it was used in the Spanish Inquisition, it was used in Pol Pot's genocide in Cambodia, and there are reports that it is being used against Buddhist monks today."*

Several days earlier, while speaking at a political rally at Dordt College in Sioux Center Iowa,[45] he again denounced waterboarding as "clear-cut torture" and said:

39   Michael B Mukasey became US AG in October 2007, succeeding Alberto R Gonzales, who resigned in the midst of investigations into the firings of federal prosecutors.

40   The Attorney General represents the United States in legal matters generally and gives advice and opinions to the President and the heads of the executive departments of the US government when so requested.

41   The Judiciary Committee's jurisdiction has broadened from criminal justice to include terrorism, human rights, immigration law, intellectual property rights, anti-trust law, and Internet privacy. The Committee is also tasked with considering the President's nominees for federal judgeships, including Supreme Court justices, as well as providing oversight of the Department of Justice, including the Federal Bureau of Investigation.

42   Shenon, Philip: "Panel Pushes Nominee to Denounce Technique." *New York Times*, October 24 2007, accessed at http://www.nytimes.com/2007/10/24/washington/24mukasey.html?ref=us.

43   John McCain, then a Lt. Commander in the Navy, was shot down and captured by the North Vietnamese in October 1967 and held for five-and-a-half years as a POW in the infamous "Hanoi Hilton."

44   Cooper, Michael and Santora, Marc: "McCain Rebukes Giuliani on Waterboarding Remark." *New York Times*, October 26 2007, accessed at http://www.nytimes.com/2007/10/26/us/politics/26giuliani.html?ref=politics#.

45   Shakir, Faiz: "McCain Calls Waterboarding 'A Horrible Torture Technique' but Will He Vote Against Mukasey?" Think Progress Security website; October 26 2007, accessed at http://thinkprogress.org/security/2007/10/26/17210/mccain-mukasey-torture/.

"People who have worn the uniform and had the experience know that this is a terrible and odious practice and should never be condoned in the U.S. We are a better nation than that."

As a victim of torture himself, McCain had no doubt that his country was guilty of torture; despite his protests, however, his colleagues in the Republican Party appeared unruffled by the implication that torture was being carried out on a number of terror suspects.

Despite the public furore, five years later, the Bush Administration had approved 2,002 EITs; by doing so, it had rewritten the rules, according to the editors[46] of the weighty book *The Torture Papers,*[47] a collection of hundreds of the so-called "Torture Memos."

The volume of documents contained within the 1,250 pages of the hardback edition presented for the first time a compilation of documents, memos and notes regarding the Bush Administration and intelligence agencies' concerns over the harsh interrogation techniques being used.

The opening lines explaining the content of formerly classified documents are as follows:

"The memos and reports in this volume document the systematic attempt of the U.S. Government to authorize the way for torture techniques and coercive interrogation practices, forbidden under international law, with the concurrent express intent of evading liability in the aftermath of any discovery of these practices and policies."

The Torture Papers had a polarising effect and triggered debates in the West over the definitions of torture when the book was published in 2005. In the introduction,

---

46   The editors: Karen J. Greenburg is Executive Director of the Center on Law & Security at New York University School of Law and editor of the NYU Review of Law & Security. Joshua L. Dratel is President of the New York State Association of Criminal Defense Lawyers, serving on Board of Directors of the National Association of Criminal Defense Lawyers.

47   Greenburg, Karen J and Dratel, Joshua L: *The Torture Papers: The Road to Abu Ghraib.* Cambridge University Press, 2005.

Anthony Lewis[48] referred to how government lawyers created a climate that, in his view, went on to lay the road to Abu Ghraib prison.[49]

While the classified memos of 2002 had, as Lewis put it *"sought to argue away the rules of torture,"* nothing could have prepared the Bush Administration for the fallout from Abu Ghraib.

Hundreds of photographs and a number of videos seized by the US Army's internal investigations team recorded three months of detainee abuse involving torture and death. So-called trophy pictures showed soldiers posing next to the body of a dead Iraqi later identified as Manadel al-Jamadi, whose body was stored by CIA personnel overnight in a shower room at Abu Ghraib. While the merits of waterboarding as a method of torture were still under debate, there was no doubt that torture had been carried out on detainees at this Baghdad prison and that their tormentors were military police personnel of the US Army, together with additional US government agencies – specifically the CIA.[50]

However, during a press conference in May 2004, US Secretary of Defence Donald Rumsfeld denied that torture had been carried out on detainees at Abu Ghraib.[51] He said: *"What has been charged so far is abuse, which I believe technically is different from torture. I'm not going to address the 'torture' word."*

He did almost reluctantly address the use of the word "torture" in his autobiography[52] when he revealed how he submitted his resignation over the Abu Ghraib scandal. It is clear from the following passage, however, that the former Defense Secretary was still irritated by the use of the word "torture" and its use in reference to the activities of the Bush Administration.

---

48   Anthony Lewis was an award-winning journalist and intellectual who wrote for T*he New York Times and The New York Review of Books*, among other publications.

49   Abu Ghraib prison in Iraq first came to public attention in 2004 after a series of photographs and videos revealed human rights violations in the form of physical, psychological and sexual abuse, including torture and reports of rape, sodomy and the murder of prisoners held in the prison.

50   On the night of Nov. 4 2003, the military police logbook in the military intelligence wing at Abu Ghraib contained this entry: "Shift change normal relief 1 OGA in 1B shower not to be used until OGA is moved out." OGA stands for "other government agency" and at Abu Ghraib, OGA referred "almost exclusively" to the Central Intelligence Agency, according to an investigation by Maj. Gen. George R Fay.

51   Hochschild, Adam: "What's in a Word? Torture." *New York Times*, May 23 2004, published in its Opinion Pages.

52   Rumsfeld: *Known and Unknown.*

"As much as I believed I was right to resign, I eventually accepted the President's decision to stay and continue to manage the scandal, while working to keep the Pentagon, two wars, and our major transformation efforts moving forward. I now believe that this was a misjudgment on my behalf. Abu Ghraib and its follow-on effects, including the continued drumbeat of 'torture' maintained by partisan critics of the war and the President, became a damaging distraction."[53]

His refusal to see Abu Ghraib as a byproduct of the decision to introduce EITs following the arrest in 2002 of Abu Zubaydah is clear from his memoirs but others dispute his insistence that Abu Ghraib had *"nothing whatsoever to do with interrogation or intelligence gathering."[54]*

There were those in government who believed the dots could be connected between the reactions to 9/11 and what emerged in Abu Ghraib. For example, Senator Carl Levin wrote:[55]

"On September 16, 2001, Vice President Dick Cheney suggested that the United States turn to the 'dark side' in our response to 9/11. Not long after that, after White House Counsel Alberto Gonzales called parts of the Geneva Conventions 'quaint,' President Bush determined that provisions of the Geneva Conventions did not apply to certain detainees. Other senior officials followed the President and Vice President's lead, authorizing policies that included harsh and abusive interrogation techniques."

Levin responded to a 230-page declassified report[56] by writing this Op-Ed for the online newspaper The Huffington Post[57] and concluded his response with the following:

"With last week's release of the Department of Justice Office of Legal Counsel (OLC) opinions, it is now widely known that Bush administration officials distorted Survival Evasion Resistance and Escape "SERE" training—a legitimate program used by the military to train our troops to resist abusive enemy interrogations—by authorizing

---

53   Rumsfeld: *Known and Unknown*, p. 551.

54   Rumsfeld: *Known and Unknown*, p. 552.

55   Democratic US Senator from Michigan and Senate Armed Services Committee Chair.

56   "Inquiry into the Treatment of Detainees in U.S. Custody." Report by the Committee on Armed Services, United States Senate, November 20 2008; declassified in April 2009.

57   Levin, Carl: "New Report: Bush Officials Tried to Shift Blame for Detainee Abuse to Low-Ranking Soldiers," *Huffington Post*, April 21 2009, accessed at http://www.huffingtonpost.com/sen-carl-levin/new-report-bush-officials_b_189823.html.

abusive techniques from SERE for use in detainee interrogations. Those decisions conveyed the message that abusive treatment was appropriate for detainees in U.S. custody."

Despite the continued furore, it is now in doubt[58] whether anyone will ever be prosecuted in a US court for carrying out harsh interrogations on terror suspects, even if they were deemed to involve torture as defined by the UN, WHO and various human rights groups.

US President Barack Obama officially announced that his administration would not prosecute CIA operatives for carrying out these controversial interrogations of terrorist suspects. He made his decision as the Justice Department began releasing a number of detailed memos describing harsh techniques used against al-Qaeda suspects in secret overseas prisons.[59]

The first memo, to the attention of John Rizzo,[60] dated August 1 2002 from Jay S Bybee,[61] was 18 pages long, marked "Top Secret" and Acting Counsel of CIA, and headed: "Interrogation of al-Qaeda Operative."

The second memo of 21 pages was from the office of the Principal Deputy Assistant Attorney General Steven G Bradbury,[62] dated May 10 2005, to the attention of John Rizzo to discuss the "Combined use of certain techniques in the interrogation of high value al-Qaeda detainees." Again, it was marked "Top Secret."

The third memo, dated May 30 2005, was again for the attention of Rizzo from Bradbury; the 40-page Top Secret document was in reference to "Application of the United States Obligations Under Article 16 of the Convention Against Torture to Certain Techniques that May Be Used in the Interrogation of High-Value al-Qaeda Detainees."

---

58   "Statement of President Barack Obama on Release of OLC Memos," issued from the Office of the Press Secretary, the White House, April 16 2009.

59   Memo 1 for John Rizzo, Acting Counsel of CIA re: Interrogation of al-Qaeda Operative from Jay S Bybee.

60   A CIA lawyer from 1976 until 2011, often credited with approving the CIA's most controversial programmes.

61   Jay S Bybee was Assistant Attorney General in 2002.

62   Bradbury was head of the Office of Legal Counsel (OLC) in the US Department of Justice during the Bush administration. He was appointed the Principal Deputy Assistant Attorney General for OLC in April 2004 and became the Acting Assistant Attorney General in 2005.

The fourth memo, dated May 30 2005, contained 40 pages for Rizzo from Bradbury on the legal authorization for a list of specific and harsh techniques, including pushing detainees against a wall, facial slaps, cramped confinement, stress positions, sleep deprivation and waterboarding.

A more pressing concern for the CIA, as indicated by a New York Times report,[63] was that the revelations could trigger a full-blown investigation into Bush Administration counter-terrorism programmes, resulting in possible torture prosecutions.

President Obama condemned what he called a *"dark and painful chapter in our history"* and revealed that these interrogation techniques would never be used again. He also repeated his opposition to a lengthy investigation, however, saying: *"nothing will be gained by spending our time and energy laying blame for the past."*

Although Obama said that CIA officers who were acting on the Justice Department's legal advice would not be prosecuted, he left open the possibility that anyone who acted without legal authorisation could still face criminal penalties. He did not address whether lawyers who authorised the use of these interrogation techniques should face retribution.

The fact remains that all legal opinions on interrogation were overturned by Obama on his second day in office, when he also outlawed harsh interrogations and ordered the closure of the CIA's secret prisons. His Executive Order 13491 on ensuring lawful interrogations states in full that torture will not be tolerated.[64]

It is slightly depressing to discover in the later chapters of this book that while this executive order may have been observed and followed elsewhere, Guantanamo detainees claim that torture continued for them, according to ex-GTMO Shaker Aamer on his release in October 2015.

Aamer even likened his experiences as a US captive to those endured by Japanese POWs after reading "Unbroken" by Laura Hillenbrand. The book is based on the World War II experiences of Louis Zamperini, a former Olympic runner who

---

63   Mazzetti, Mark and Shane, Scott: "Interrogation Memos Detail Harsh Tactics by the CIA." *New York Times*, April 16 2009.

64   Executive Order 13491 – "Ensuring Lawful Interrogations," January 22 2009.

joined the US Army Air Force as a young lieutenant. He was captured and held by the Japanese until the end of the war.

One passage on the Japanese propaganda and racism directed towards captives which resonated with Shaker Aamer was the following: *"… Japanese soldiers and civilians, intensely propagandized by their government, usually carried out their own caustic prejudices about their enemies, seeing them as brutish, subhuman beasts or fearsome 'Anglo-Saxon Devils.' This racism, and the hatred and fear it fomented, surely served as an accelerant for abuse of Allied prisoners … Some guards, intoxicated by absolute power and indoctrinated in racism and disgust for POWs, fell easily into sadism … To be made responsible for imprisoning people is surely, to many guards, an unsettling experience, especially when they are tasked with depriving their prisoners of the most basic necessities. Perhaps some guards forced their prisoners to live in maximally dehumanizing conditions so that they could reassure themselves that they were merely giving loathsome beasts their due. Paradoxically, then, some of the worst abuses inflicted on captives and POWs may have arisen from the guards' discomfort with being abusive."*[65]

In another chapter, the author goes into detail about the Japanese torture of one POW, which included waterboarding using a similar method to that of the CIA. It reads as follows:

"The Japanese had attempted, in vain, to torture information out of [John] Fitzgerald, clubbing him, jamming penknives under his fingernails, tearing his fingernails off, and applying the 'water cure' – tipping him backward, holding his mouth shut, and pouring water up his nose until he passed out."[66]

President Obama's Presidential Order sought to end the official government debate on what constituted torture, but it is an argument that continues unabated today. However, Obama's definitions made clear that future interrogation techniques deployed by military and other intelligence agencies must not involve torture as defined at the beginning of this chapter within the Geneva Conventions and UNCAT.

Obama's order was clearly at odds with the previous administration's views and definitions, but at the time of this book's publication, no one had been legally challenged in an official court of law about the way in which the Bush

---

65   Hillenbrand, Laura: *Unbroken*. London, Fourth Estate, 2010, p. 201–202.
66   Hillenbrand: *Unbroken*, p. 207.

Administration had reinterpreted those definitions, although symbolic courts without jurisdiction have issued war crimes rulings in Malaysia.

In 2011, the first of the Kuala Lumpur War Crimes Tribunals (KLWCT),[67] established in 2007 by former Malaysian PM Mahathir Mohamad,[68] found President George W Bush and former Prime Minister Tony Blair both guilty of war crimes and ruled *"that Bush and Blair's name(s) should be entered in a register of war criminals."* The judges urged that their findings be recognised as such under the ICC Rome Statute, and also petitioned the International Criminal Court "to proceed with binding charges."[69]

As mentioned in the opening chapter, the KLWCT has received a mixed reception and while it is supported by anti-war movements, its legitimacy is criticised by others since it lacks a UN mandate. Tribunal president Tan Sri Dato Lamin Bin Haji Mohd Yunus Lamin admitted as much at the hearing in Kuala Lumpur at which President Bush and his key advisers were convicted in absentia as war criminals for torture and cruel, inhumane and degrading treatment. At the conclusion of the hearing in May 2012, he said:

> *"The tribunal has no power of enforcement, no power to impose any custodial sentence on any one or more of the 8 convicted persons. What we can do, under Article 31 of Chapter VI of Part 2 of the Charter, is to recommend to the Kuala Lumpur War Crimes Commission to submit this finding of conviction by the Tribunal, together with a record of these proceedings, to the Chief Prosecutor of the International Criminal Court, as well as the United Nations and the Security Council."*

At the 2012 tribunal, George W Bush, Dick Cheney, Donald Rumsfeld, Alberto Gonzales, David Addington, William J Haynes II, Jay S Bybee and John Yoo were found guilty of the crime of torture. Lamin noted:

> *"The Accused had wilfully participated in the formulation of executive orders and directives to exclude the applicability of international conventions and laws – namely*

---

67   The tribunal is part of the Kuala Lumpur Foundation to Criminalise War (KLFCW), a non-governmental organization established on March 12 2007. Its stated intention is to undertake "all necessary measures and initiatives to criminalise war and energise peace."

68   Mahathir Mohamad is founder and chairman of KLFCW. In 1981 he became the fourth Prime Minister of Malaysia, serving until 2003.

69   The KLWCT also unanimously found George W Bush and Tony Blair guilty of "crimes against peace" in 2010.

the UN Convention against Torture (1984), the Geneva Conventions (1949), the Universal Declaration of Human Rights and the United Nations Charter – "in relation to the war launched by the US and others in Afghanistan in 2001 and Iraq in March 2003," and also that "Additionally, and/or on the basis and in furtherance thereof, the accused authorized, or connived in, the commission of acts of torture and cruel, degrading and inhumane treatment against victims in violation of international law, treaties and aforesaid conventions."[70]

The ruling, like that of November 2011, is not enforceable legally, but the transcripts of the charges, witness statements and other relevant material were sent to the chief prosecutor of the International Criminal Court as well as the United Nations and the UN Security Council as a matter of record.

While visiting Kuala Lumpur for the tribunal, I challenged Professor Francis Boyle,[71] part of the prosecution team, over the legitimacy of the court and its judgement; he responded by quoting a section of the Nuremberg Charter stating the following:

"Leaders, organizers, instigators and accomplices participating in the formulation or execution of a common plan or conspiracy to commit war crimes are responsible for all acts performed by any person in execution of such a plan and the US is subject to customary international law and to the Principles of the Nuremberg Charter."

He made it clear that he was as convinced of the moral legitimacy of the war crimes tribunal and its findings in the same robust fashion as the conviction displayed by some members of the Bush Administration as set out in their various autobiographies, wherein they too claim moral legitimacy for their actions.

As the next chapter will show, however, while American politicians put on a united front for the outside world, there was much angst and deliberation behind the scenes among key members of the Bush Administration over the use of EITs performed on so-called enemy combatants caught up in the GWOT.

---

70   The full report can be found on the website of the KLFCW, accessed at http://criminalisewar. org/.

71   Boyle, a professor of international law at the University of Illinois College of Law, advises numerous international bodies in the areas of human rights, war crimes and genocide.

According to recollections published in Dick Cheney's memoirs,[72] he said the following:

> *"Since the beginning of the enhanced interrogation program, the CIA had briefed key members of Congress on the interrogations and on what they were learning. I do not recall in any of the briefings I attended a single member objecting to the program or urging that we stop using these authorized legal methods."*

---

72   Cheney: *In My Time.* For more, see: Hayes, Stephen F: *Cheney: The Untold Story of America's Most Powerful and Controversial Vice President.* New York, HarperCollins, 2007; and Gellman Barton: *Angler: The Cheney Vice Presidency.* New York, Penguin Press, 2008.

3
Political Angst Behind the Scenes

Although the issue of legality is not essential to this work, it might still be useful to look at some of the so-called "Torture Memos" penned by the legal team advising the Bush Administration. This is because that administration invested so much time and effort on how the law would shape and justify their argument for using harsh interrogation techniques. While some close supporters of the President, including Senator John McCain,[1] considered that EITs involved torture and should be banned, it is obvious that key officials, including President Bush himself, believed torture could and would work.

This fact is illustrated in Bush's memoirs, when he recalls, in a particularly reflective moment, the accomplishments and criticisms of his two-term Presidency as he was about to leave office. In this passage, he lays out a brief defence for using these controversial interrogation techniques while also summing up his greatest achievements:[2]

> "I have been troubled by the blowback against the intelligence community and Justice Department for their role in the surveillance and interrogation programs. Our intelligence officers carried out their orders with skill and courage, and they deserve our gratitude for protecting our nation. Legal officials in my administration did their best to resolve the complex issues in a time of extraordinary danger to our country … After the nightmare of September 11, America went seven and a half years without another successful terrorist attack on our soil. If I had to summarize my most meaningful accomplishment as president in one sentence, that would be it."

It is significant that Bush regarded the controversy over the use of EITs as indelibly linked with his most *"meaningful accomplishment,"* as if to emphasise that one could not be achieved without the other while also invoking the memory of 9/11.

His Vice President's memoirs include similar passages justifying the use of torture and citing the crucial support of the legal side of the Bush Administration; in

---

1   McCain proved to be a particularly powerful adversary because he was a decorated war hero as well as a Republican who had endured torture for five years as a POW during the Vietnam War.

2   Bush: *Decision Points*, p. 180–181.

this passage referring to HVD KSM, Cheney recalls political moves on Capitol Hill in 2005 to return to the Army Field Manual 3-24 guidelines and end the EIT programme, which he says had been providing *"invaluable intelligence:"*[3]

> *"But a detainee such as Khalid Sheikh Mohammed is different. He wasn't talking, but there was no one comparable to move on to. For the safety of the nation we needed him to talk, and that happened after we put him through the enhanced interrogation program."*

As I will set out in this chapter, the President's men – and women – were satisfied with giving the go ahead for the enhanced interrogations on HVDs following comprehensive advice from lawyers, having convinced themselves that torture would produce results.

That the legal advice took several months to formulate, from the arrest of Abu Zubaydah to the implementing of the EITs, may come as a surprise to critics who thought the process was set in motion with a flurry of phone and conference calls within days. However, the questions that still loom large are these: Did the harsh, CIA-led interrogations of Abu Zubaydah, KSM and the other detainees work? If so, which method in the list of EITs proved to be the most effective, and what were the results? Would it be enough to silence the growing army of critics who described EITs as both torture and ineffective?

In the wake of 9/11, the Bush Administration brought in many sweeping changes via legislation, including the Patriot Act[4] designed to make life easier for US intelligence agencies – including the CIA, FBI and the law enforcement agencies – to combat terrorism.

Such was the climate of political cooperation following the attacks in September 2001 that politicians from across all parties gave their support and the Act passed into law by huge bipartisan majorities in October of that year.

The US Department of Justice website describes the key role played by the Patriot Act as follows:

---

3   Cheney, Dick: *In My Time*. New York, Threshold, 2011, p. 359.
4   Department of Justice website, accessed at http://www.justice.gov/archive/ll/highlights. htm.

"Since its passage following the September 11, 2001 attacks, the Patriot Act has played a key part – and often the leading role – in a number of successful operations to protect innocent Americans from the deadly plans of terrorists dedicated to destroying America and our way of life. While the results have been important, in passing the Patriot Act, Congress provided for only modest, incremental changes in the law. Congress simply took existing legal principles and retrofitted them to preserve the lives and liberty of the American people from the challenges posed by a global terrorist network."

Investigating and combatting terrorist activities became the number one priority for both intelligence and law enforcement agencies, according to Karl Rove's autobiography[5] "Courage and Consequence," in which he reveals the inner workings of the Bush Administration during the events of 2001.

Rove, a senior adviser to the US President from 2000 to 2007 and his Deputy Chief of Staff from 2004 to 2007, writes how Bush:

"… established the position of Director of National Intelligence and instructed our nation's intelligence agencies to create a layered system that could nab terrorists overseas, at the border, and within the country. Bush set up a national Counter-terrorism Center where federal, state, and local department and agency personnel would work side by side to track terrorist threats."

However, Rove is keen to stress that of all the new legislation and agencies put in place after 9/11, none was as controversial as the Bush decision to authorise the use of EITs.[6] He also is keen to stress that he was not aware of the programme at the time, so secret were its contents.

In his chapter "Striking Back," as he outlines all of the new legislation, Rove reveals that: *"no issue became as controversial as when the president – unbeknownst to me at the time – authorized the use of enhanced interrogation techniques (EITs) on high-value terrorist detainees."* [7]

---

5   Rove, Karl: *Courage and Consequence: My Life as a Conservative in the Fight*. New York, Simon and Schuster, 2010, p. 294–297.

6   Techniques authorised by the Bush administration for use by the CIA and Department of Defense to extract information from terror suspects in the wake of 9/11.

7   Rove: *Courage and Consequence*, Ch. 18, p. 295.

This chapter will look at exactly what EITs involved, now that the definitions of torture have been established in the previous chapter. That someone as close to the US President as Rove insists that he did not know of the existence of EITs in those early days gives an indication of how sensitive was the decision to employ such tactics. We now know they were officially authorised in August 2002, according to Rove.

He describes them as: *"These tough, coercive techniques included stress positions, cramped confinement, 'insult slaps,' dietary manipulation, wall standing, water dousings, sleep deprivation, and waterboarding."*

The whole issue went on to become a major topic for debate, as it still is, so it is thus not surprising that the subject of EITs surfaces in the pages of Bush's autobiography "Decision Points".[8] The US President recalls in his chapter "War Footing" how the capture of the HVD and al-Qaeda suspect Abu Zubaydah in March 2002 triggered and accelerated the issue of EITs. He writes as follows:

"The FBI began questioning Zubaydah, who had clearly been trained on how to resist interrogation. He revealed bits and pieces of information that he thought we already knew. Frighteningly, we didn't know much ... Then Zubaydah stopped answering questions. George Tenet[9] told me interrogators believed Zubaydah had more intelligence to reveal. If he was hiding something more, what could it be? Zubaydah was our best lead to avoid another catastrophic attack. 'We need to find out what he knows,' I directed the team. 'What are our options?'"

Those options included moving him to another country where the CIA would have total control over his environment. In the meantime, CIA experts drew up a list of techniques yet to be tried on the captive. Bush says he was reassured by George Tenet and, in the same passage, continues in this way:

"... all interrogations would be performed by experienced intelligence professionals who had undergone extensive training. Medical personnel would be on-site to guarantee that the detainee was not physically or mentally harmed.

---

8   Bush: *Decision Points*, p. 168–169.

9   George John Tenet was Director of Central Intelligence from July 1997–July 2004.

"At my direction, the Department of Justice and CIA lawyers conducted a careful legal review. They concluded that the enhanced interrogation program complied with the Constitution and all applicable laws, including those that ban torture.

"I took a look at the list of techniques. There were two that I felt went too far, even if they were legal. I directed the CIA not to use them. Another technique was waterboarding, a process of simulated drowning. No doubt the procedure was tough, but medical experts assured the CIA that it did no lasting harm."

Revealingly, Bush again justifies his actions by saying he sought legal advice and consulted medical experts before reaching a decision. Could the US President have been using his advisers as a legal defensive shield? Rather tellingly, Bush concedes he knew that one day this decision-making process and issue would become public and he would have to account for and justify his actions. Once again invoking the raw memories of 9/11, he says:

"Had I not authorized waterboarding on senior al-Qaeda leaders, I would have had to accept a greater risk that the country would be attacked. In the wake of 9/11, that was a risk I was unwilling to take. My most solemn responsibility as president was to protect the country. I approved the use of the interrogation techniques."[10]

It is a view shared by Bush's inner circle.[11] As revealed in all of their autobiographies as outlined below, the defining moment for the consideration of introducing harsher interrogation techniques came with the arrest of Abu Zubaydah.

Vice President Cheney recalls events following a raid in March 2002 of an al-Qaeda safe house in Faisalabad, Pakistan leading to the capture of Abu Zubaydah:[12]

"A lieutenant of Osama bin Laden, Zubaydah was the highest ranking al Qaeda member we had captured to date ... Although defiant, Zubaydah provided useful information very early on, disclosing, for example, that the mastermind behind 9/11 had been Khalid Sheikh Mohammed, or KSM. He also provided KSM's code name, Mukhtar. But then he stopped answering questions, and

the CIA, convinced he had information that could potentially save thousands of lives, approached the Justice Department and the White House about what they might do to go further in interrogating him and other high-value detainees. The CIA developed a list of enhanced interrogation techniques that were based on the Survival, Evasion, Resistance, and Escape program used to prepare our military men and women in case they should be captured, detained, or interrogated. Before using the techniques on any terrorists, the CIA wanted the Justice Department to review them, and determine that they complied with the law, including international treaty obligations such as the United Nations Convention Against Torture."

Cheney is at pains to note that the whole procedure took some months, a point former Secretary of State Condoleezza Rice reinforced in her autobiography, published in the same year. She writes of Zubaydah's capture:[13]

"The intelligence agencies and those who were interrogating him were certain that he knew far more than he was letting on, perhaps even crucial information about impending plots. It was under those circumstances that the Central Intelligence Agency sought authorization to use particular procedures they referred to as 'enhanced interrogation techniques.' The President asked two questions: Would the proposed interrogation program be legal? Is it necessary?"

Rice, who was the National Security Advisor (NSA) at the time, says in her book that the suspect was *"key"* to understanding impending plots, and she asked for Secretary of Defense Donald Rumsfeld to be briefed together with then US Secretary of State Colin Powell.[14]

The whole process of answering the US President's two questions about *"necessity"* and *"legality"* took some months and went through his highest-level advisers,[15] according to Rice. She recalls that in the meantime the CIA was put on standby to begin the EIT program at a moment's notice.

---

13   Rice: *No Higher Honour*, p. 117–121.
14   Colin Powell, a retired four-star general, was the 65th US Secretary of State, serving from 2001–2005.
15   Rice: *No Higher Honour*, p. 118: "I had asked the Attorney General to review this case personally. The President needed that confirmation from the nation's top legal officer, not just the lawyers in the Office of Legal Counsel."

Rice points out that although Zubaydah had been captured on March 22 2002,[16] the full authorisation did not come through until August, perhaps to illustrate that a great deal of soul searching had taken place and legal advice carefully scrutinised before the final decision was made.

This issue was revealed in matching detail by CIA head George Tenet[17] in his autobiography.[18] Again, he says that the input from lawyers was key to the justification for using EITs. Until the capture of Zubaydah, Tenet admits he was disappointed by the low-quality information available from detainees who were either *"too low ranking"* or *"too disciplined"* to reveal *"useful information."* However, that all changed with the arrival of Zubaydah:

> *"But Zubaydah and a small number of other extremely highly placed terrorists potentially had information that might save thousands of lives. We wondered what we could legitimately do to get that information. Despite what Hollywood might have you believe, in situations like this you don't call in the tough guys; you call in the lawyers. It took until August to get clear guidance on what Agency officers could legally do."[19]*

There is a slight departure or discrepancy in Donald Rumsfeld's account when he recalls the capture and interrogation procedures agreed upon regarding Zubaydah.[20] Rumsfeld, Defense Secretary at the time, writes:

> *"As a member of the National Security Council, I was made aware of the Agency's interrogation program—but as I now understand it, it was not until well after it had been initiated, and well after the senior members of the congressional intelligence committees in Congress, including future Speaker of the House Nancy Pelosi and others had been briefed. Along with my colleagues on the NSC I learned that the CIA had developed a series of enhanced techniques to achieve Zubaydah's cooperation."*

However, as mentioned previously, Condaleezza Rice wrote in her autobiography how she specifically insisted that Rumsfeld and Powell "be briefed" on the

---

16   Rice: *No Higher Honour*, p. 116.

17   George Tenet was Director of Central Intelligence from 1997–2004.

18   Tenet, George: *At the Center of the Storm*. New York, HarperCollins, 2007.

19   Tenet: *At the Center of the Storm*, p. 241.

20   Rumsfeld: *Known and Unknown*, p. 583.

Zubaydah debate over the proposed use of EITs.[21] Either her instructions were ignored or she and Rumsfeld have different recollections.

At the time of writing their memoirs, Rumsfeld and his colleagues who served in the Bush Administration would have been acutely aware of attempts by human rights groups to have arrest warrants for torture issued in their names.[22]

Thus, perhaps it is not surprising they would want to distance themselves from any of the specific decision making over the use of EITs, which some regarded as being defined as torture and therefore illegal under international law. Each autobiography clearly puts the responsibility on the shoulders of lawyers; however, the targeting of key members of the Bush Administration began in earnest[23] several years after the opening of the Guantanamo Bay detention centre, the invasion of Iraq and revelations of CIA ghost prisons[24] and rendition[25] flights.

In 2005, US Secretary of Defense Donald Rumsfeld was threatened with arrest in Germany for war crimes relating to abuses in Iraq. Rumsfeld was cited in a 384-page document sitting on the German Federal Prosecutor's desk,[26] causing a diplomatic headache for the German government.

The lawsuit was filed by Berlin-based lawyer Wolfgang Kaleck,[27] according to an article in Der Spiegel,[28] which named others, including Alberto Gonzales, then

21   Rice: *No Higher Honour*, p. 117, "I asked that Colin and Don be briefed."

22   Duff, Gordon: "Bush 'Blood Money' Tour Cancelled," *Veterans Today, Journal for the Clandestine Community*, Feb 6 2011, accessed at http://www.veteranstoday. com/2011/02/06/gordon-duff-bush-blood-money-tour-cancelled/.

23   MacAskill, Ewan and Hirsch, Afua: "George Bush Calls Off Trip to Switzerland." *The Guardian*, February 7 2011, p. 14, main section.

24   Ghost prisons, also known as black sites, refer to secret detention centres run by the CIA, as referred to in a David Williams Daily Mail.com. story, accessed at http://www.dailymail. co.uk/news/article-460749/CIA-ran-secret-ghost-prisons-terror-suspects-Europe.html.

25   "Rendition" means the practice of covertly sending a foreign criminal or terrorist suspect to be interrogated in a country with less rigorous regulations for the humane treatment of prisoners, according to Oxford Dictionaries online, accessed at http://oxforddictionaries. com/definition/rendition?region=us.

26   Demmer, Ulrike: "Rumsfeld Lawsuit Embarrasses German Authorities." Spiegel Online International, March 26 2007, accessed at http://www.spiegel.de/international/ world/0,1518,473987,00.html.

27   Wolfgang Kaleck is a German civil rights attorney. He is also the General Secretary for the European Center for Constitutional and Human Rights.

28   Der Spiegel is a German weekly news magazine published in Hamburg; it has an international online version, http://www.spiegel.de.

Attorney General; CIA head George Tenet; and Lieutenant General Ricardo S Sanchez, the US general who served as the commander of coalition forces in Iraq from June 2003 to June 2004. According to the document, these members of the US elite violated both international law and the United Nations Convention Against Torture in Abu Ghraib[29] prison and the Guantanamo Bay detention camp.

Charges were dismissed after it was decided that Germany's criminal prosecution of the accused would lead to an infringement of the international principles of subsidiarity and non-intervention in the affairs of foreign states (comity). An appeal was lodged but this petition was also unsuccessful and eventually the higher regional court of Baden-Wurttemberg in Stuttgart dismissed this as inadmissible.

On November 14 2006, another criminal charge was filed against Rumsfeld (who had resigned several days earlier on November 8) and 13 other individuals on behalf of 44 individuals and organizations. This new criminal charge alleged the commission of war crimes and acts of torture by the United States in its detention facilities in Abu Ghraib and Guantanamo Bay, Cuba. The accused in this case were not only state and military officers, as was the case in the first complaint, but also former government lawyers for their culpability for the actions of their government.

The German federal prosecutor once again dismissed this criminal charge, citing similar considerations as in his February 2005 decision; this leaves the Rumsfeld case to serve as another example of the so far unsuccessful judicial implementation of the German Code of Crimes against International Law of 2002.

The key members of the Bush Administration, and even Bush himself, obviously had premonitions of the furore the decision making over EIT might provoke in the future, and their fears were borne out, although by early 2016 all legal attempts had failed to result into court appearances.

Rumsfeld dwells on this issue in his autobiography but, interestingly, he is also keen for it to be known that while the intelligence agencies had developed EITs, it was something to which he denied the military intelligence access, even though

---

29   Abu Ghraib prison in Iraq (also known as Baghdad Correctional Facility) first came to public attention in 2004 following human rights violations and torture committed by US military and government agencies.

the Justice Department *"had determined that the interrogation techniques the CIA was using—up to and including waterboarding—were legal."*[30]

Rumsfeld cites his reasons:[31]

"Though the CIA utilized waterboarding and other techniques that I had rejected in the Department of Defense, I saw no contradiction. Some techniques that might be appropriate for a very small number of high-value terrorists by a highly trained and professional group of CIA interrogators in a controlled environment were not appropriate for use by military personnel. It would have been unwise to blur the difference between two distinct institutions. Tight limits on interrogation, such as those contained in the Army Field Manual, are appropriate for the U.S. military. Tens of thousands of detainees passed through U.S. military custody in Afghanistan and Iraq. Conversely, the CIA was dealing with a small number of key terrorist leaders believed to be senior al-Qaida operatives. CIA personnel were trained to use enhanced interrogation tactics in carefully monitored situations. We didn't want young military personnel making decisions on interrogating high-level al-Qaida terrorists."

What has been established so far is that the Bush Administration adopted an extremely cautious approach towards the CIA request to introduce the use of EITs among its high-value detainees following the capture of Zubaydah in March 2002.

In addition, while the practice was forbidden in the US military, EITs were put in use on Zubaydah by specially trained CIA officers in September 2002; he would, according to one former FBI agent,[32] become the guinea pig for them.

It is perhaps interesting to note that more than 13 years on, by the close of 2015, Zubaydah had not been charged with a single crime,[33] which begs the question of his credibility and importance as an HVD. In the meantime, he is still being held in Guantanamo without trial or charge.

---

30   Rumsfeld: *Known and Unknown*, p. 583.
31   Rumsfeld: *Known and Unknown*, p. 584.
32   Ali Soufan joined the FBI in the 1990s and, as one of the only Arabic speakers, was assigned to Zubaydah's interrogation sessions. This download reveals details of the interrogations to BBC Newsnight journalists on September 12 2011, accessed at http://www.bbc.co.uk/news/world-us-canada-14891439.
33   Accessed at http://www.reprieve.org.uk/case-study/abu-zubaydah/.

The use of EITs remained top secret until ABC News[34] ran a story in which they claimed that in November 2005[35] CIA sources had given them a list of six EITs instituted in mid-March 2002 and used, they said, on a dozen top al-Qaeda targets held in isolation at ghost prisons in regions from Asia to Eastern Europe. According to the sources, only 14 CIA interrogators were trained in EITs.

The news channel's exclusive was regarded by the wider media as sensational and was duly followed by other print and broadcast outlets, including the BBC.[36] Thus, the controversial EITs were broadcast to the public for the first time and listed as set out below:[37]

1. The Attention Grab: The interrogator forcefully grabs the shirt front of the prisoner and shakes him.

2. Attention Slap: An open-handed slap aimed at causing pain and triggering fear.

3. The Belly Slap: A hard open-handed slap to the stomach. The aim is to cause pain, but not internal injury. Doctors consulted advised against using a punch, which could cause lasting internal damage.

4. Long Time Standing: This technique is described as among the most effective. Prisoners are forced to stand, handcuffed and with their feet shackled to an eye bolt in the floor, for more than 40 hours. Exhaustion and sleep deprivation are effective in yielding confessions.

5. The Cold Cell: The prisoner is left to stand naked in a cell kept near 50 degrees Fahrenheit. Throughout the time in the cell the prisoner is doused with cold water.

---

34   ABC News is the news gathering and broadcasting division of the American Broadcasting Company.

35   Ross, Brian and Esposito, Richard: "CIA's Harsh Interrogation Techniques Described." ABC News Investigative Unit, November 18 2005, ABC News online reference, accessed at http://abcnews.go.com/WNT/Investigation/story?id=1322866#.T1VP2ZhA4so.

36   Reynolds, Paul: BBC News website, December 8 2005, "Defining Torture in a New World War," accessed at http://news.bbc.co.uk/1/hi/4499528.stm.

37   Ross, Brian and Esposito, Richard: "CIA's Harsh Interrogation Techniques Described."

6. Water Boarding: The prisoner is bound to an inclined board, feet raised and head slightly below the feet. Cellophane is wrapped over the prisoner's face and water is poured over him. Unavoidably, the gag reflex kicks in and a terrifying fear of drowning leads to almost instant pleas to bring the treatment to a halt.

To fully comprehend each point, perhaps the best description comes from Abu Zubaydah himself; he gave a lengthy account to the International Committee of the Red Cross (ICRC),[38] though his reliability as narrator can not be guaranteed on several levels. If he is an al-Qaeda terrorist, his statement could be deliberately misleading, according to Montgomery J Granger, Major (Retd),[39] who urged caution, saying:

"Remember that al-Qaeda and other captives are trained to lie about their treatment. They are specifically instructed to claim abuse and torture at the hands of their captors. I would say any statement by any detainee is suspect when mentioning torture or abuse. Not that it doesn't or didn't happen, but the reliability of such statements should not be believed out of hand.

Unlawful combatant Islamist extremists expect to be killed or tortured should they become captives. I heard this many times from detainees at GTMO, through interpreters. In fact, when we transferred detainees from Camp X-Ray to Camp Delta at GTMO in April of 2002, I witnessed every single detainee enter his new cell, along with the camp commander and an interpreter, who spoke with most detainees, several of whom were extremely agitated and confused. Many, I was told (perhaps 1/3), were convinced they were being taken to be executed."

However, if critics of EITs are right in their assessment, those subjected to torture could also make unreliable witnesses because their judgement and recollections could be impaired due to mental and physical stress. Therefore, a personal judgement call can be made with any certainty only by reading and evaluating the contents of this very personal account given by Zubaydah:[40]

---

38   The ICRC, established in 1863, works worldwide to provide humanitarian help for people affected by conflict and armed violence and to promote the laws that protect victims of war. An independent organisation, its mandate stems essentially from the Geneva Conventions of 1949. At the time of writing this book, Zubaydah had not been charged or tried with any offence.

39   Medical Service, US Army Reserve and author of Saving Grace at Guantanamo Bay; he was posted to Guantanamo in 2002 and Abu Ghraib in 2005. He was interviewed for this research via email in September 2012.

40   Cole, David: *The Torture Memos*: New York, New Press, 2009. Letter reproduced in introductory commentary.

"About two or three months after I arrived in this place, the interrogation began again, but with more intensity than before ... I was then dragged from the small box, unable to walk properly and put on what looked like a hospital bed, and strapped down very tightly with belts. A black cloth was then placed over my face and the interrogators used a mineral water bottle to pour water on the cloth so that I could not breathe. After a few minutes the cloth was removed and the bed was rotated into an upright position. The pressure of the straps on my wounds was very painful. I vomited. The bed was then again lowered to a horizontal position and the same torture carried out again with the black cloth over my face and water poured on from a bottle. On this occasion my head was in a more backward, downwards position and the water was poured on for a longer time. I struggled against the straps, trying to breathe, but it was hopeless. I thought I was going to die. I lost control of my urine. Since then I still lose control of my urine when under stress."[41]

The report eventually was leaked to author Mark Danner,[42] who republished its contents in The New York Review of Books[43] in exactly the same manner, including typographical errors and some omitted words. The text can be downloaded from the Review's website.[44]

Despite the angst displayed by key members of the Bush Administration over the use of EITs by a team of specially trained CIA interrogators, as outlined in this chapter in their own words, they all emphasise that the techniques received clearance by top legal advisers, from the Attorney General down.

However, in a letter dated February 14 2007 to John Rizzo,[45] who was Acting General Counsel of the CIA at the time, the ICRC's Head of Regional Delegation

---

41   This account by Zubaydah was first contained in an ICRC report on the "*Treatment of the Fourteen 'High-Value Detainees in CIA Custody,*" February 2007.

42   Mark Danner is Chancellor's Professor of English, Journalism and Politics at the University of California at Berkeley and James Clarke Chace Professor of Foreign Affairs, Politics and the Humanities at Bard College.

43   Danner, Mark: "*The Red Cross Torture Report: What it Means,*" The New York Review of Books, April 30 2009, p. 43.

44   An exact replica of the report can be accessed at http://www.nybooks.com/media/ doc/2010/04/22/icrc-report.pdf .

45   John Rizzo was described as the most influential career lawyer in CIA history by the Los Angeles Times in June 29 2009, accessed at http://articles.latimes.com/2009/jun/29/ nation/na-cia-lawyer29. He retired in 2009.

Geoff Loane[46] leaves no doubt as to his view of the treatments of the fourteen HVDs.[47] Marked "strictly confidential," Loane wrote as follows:

"The general term 'ill-treatment' has been used throughout the following section; however, it should in no way be understood as minimising the severity of the conditions and treatment to which the detainees were subjected. Indeed, as outlined in Section 4 below, and as concluded by this report, the ICRC clearly considers that the allegations of the fourteen include descriptions of treatment and interrogation techniques — singly or in combination — that amounted to torture and/or cruel, inhuman or degrading treatment."

The Fourteen[48] to which he refers were all subjected to EITs after they were arrested and are named as such: Abu Zubaydah, Palestinian, arrested in Pakistan on March 28 2002; Ramzi Mohammed Binalshib, Yemeni, arrested in Pakistan on September 11 2002; Abdelrahim Hussein Abdul Nashiri, Saudi, arrested in Dubai in October 2002; Mustafha Ahmad al-Hawsawi, Saudi, arrested in Pakistan on March 1 2003; Khaled Sheik Mohammed, Pakistani, arrested in Pakistan on March 1 2003; Majid Khan, Pakistani, arrested in Pakistan on March 5 2003; Ali Abdul Aziz Mohammed, Pakistani, arrested in Pakistan on April 29 2003; Walid Bin Attash, Yemeni, arrested in Pakistan on April 29 2003; Mohammed Farik Bin Amin, Malaysian, arrested in Thailand on June 8 2003; Mohammed Nazir Bin Lep, Malaysian, arrested in Thailand on August 11 2003; Encep Nuraman (aka Hambali), Indonesian, arrested in Thailand on August 11 2003; Haned Hassan Ahmad Guleed, Somali, arrested in Djibouti on March 4 2004; Ahmed Khalafan Ghailani, Tanzanian, arrested in Pakistan on July 25 2004; and Mustafah Faraj al-Azibi, Libyan, arrested in Pakistan on May 2 2005.

According to the ICRC report, these HVDs were held throughout their detention in several different places in several different countries. Prior to their arrival in Guantanamo in September 2006, the number of sites at which they had been kept ranged from between three to ten.

---

46   Geoff Loane is Head of Mission (ICRC) in London.

47   The 14 are 1) Abu Zubaydah, 2) Ramzi Mohammed Binalshib, 3) Abdelrahim Hussein Abdul Nashiri, 4) Mustafha Ahmad al-Hawsawi, 5) Khaled Shaik Mohammed, 6) Majid Khan, 7) Ali Abdul Aziz Mohammed, 8) Walid Bin Attash, 9) Mohammed Farik Bin Amin, 10) Mohammed Nazir Bin Lep, 11) Encep Nuraman (aka Hambali), 12) Haned Hassan Ahmad Guleed, 13) Ahmed Khalafan Ghailani, and 14) Mustafah Faraj al-Azibi.

48   The ICRC met with each of these detainees in private from October 6 to 11, and from December 4 to 14, 2006, several weeks after they had arrived in Guantanamo Bay.

In all cases, the detainees said they were photographed both clothed and naked prior to and again after transfer. Each flight would involve the HVD being forced to wear an adult nappy under a tracksuit. Earphones would be placed over his ears and music would occasionally be played. Each man would be blindfolded with at least a cloth tied around the head and black goggles. In addition, some detainees alleged that cotton wool was also taped over their eyes prior to the blindfold and goggles being applied.

The ICRC's confidential[49] report to Rizzo stated:

"The ICRC was informed by the US authorities that the practice of transfers was linked specifically to issues that included national security and logistics, as opposed to being an integral part of the program, for example to maintain compliance. However, in practice, these transfers increased the vulnerability of the fourteen to their interrogation, and was [were] performed in a manner (goggles, earmuffs, use of diapers, strapped to stretchers, sometimes rough handling) that was intrusive and humiliating and that challenged the dignity of the persons concerned."

The political angst over CIA activities during the ongoing GWOT continued throughout the Obama years, as was evidenced in September 2015, when US government officials blocked the release of 116 pages of defense lawyers' notes detailing the torture Abu Zubaydah says he experienced in CIA custody. The focus of speculation for years since his arrest, Zubaydah, has lost one eye and was waterboarded 83 times in a single month while held by the CIA.

"We submitted 116 pages in ten separate submissions. The government declared all of it classified," the detainee's lead defense lawyer Joe Margulies told the Reuters news agency. He and members of legal teams for the other detainees said the decision revealed that the Obama administration regarded personal accounts as classified. Could it be that the US President feared the consequences of releasing more reports, especially for US citizens living overseas?

He had, after all, agreed to the release of a 480-page executive summary in a US Senate report on CIA torture in December 2014, although some pages were still redacted. The government had also loosened its classification rules and released

---

49   The ICRC's reputation for its confidential approach to dealing with sensitive issues is internationally acknowledged; if the ICRC marks a report as confidential, it means that it is intended only for the authorities or parties to the conflict to whom it is addressed.

27 pages of interview notes compiled by lawyers for detainee Majid Khan at the same time, in which he described his torture.

Khan, a Guantanamo detainee turned government cooperating witness, said interrogators poured ice water on his genitals, twice videotaped him naked and repeatedly touched his "private parts" – none of which was described in the Senate report. He said that guards, some of whom smelled of alcohol, also threatened to beat him with a hammer, baseball bats, sticks and leather belts.

CIA and White House officials opposed releasing the Senate report, but Senator Dianne Feinstein, who then chaired the Intelligence Committee, went ahead and published the contents, which will be examined in more detail in the next chapter.

A month after the report's release, government lawyers said in a January 2015 court filing that the CIA had issued new classification rules that permitted the release of "general allegations of torture" and "information regarding the conditions of confinement." But they said the names of CIA employees or contractors could not be released and would remain secret, along with the locations of so-called "black" sites where detainees were held around the world after the 9/11 attacks.

Margulies said the 116 pages of notes he submitted for clearance were limited to Zubaydah's description of his torture and did not include prohibited information. He went on to accuse the CIA of trying to *"guarantee that Abu Zubaydah never discloses what was done to him."*

While President Obama said the contents of the redacted CIA documents had done *"significant damage to America's standing in the world,"* the CIA Director John Brennan still insists today that the practices, deemed torture by some, *"did produce intelligence that helped save lives."*

The next chapter will look in detail at the contents of the so-called CIA Torture Files and the consequences both before and after their release.

4
A Glimpse Inside Pandora's Box

Very few people outside of the CIA knew, for sure, exactly what torture—if any—had been carried out. Nor did anyone really know for sure the names of all of those interrogated and where the EIT programs were being conducted—until an official 500-page summary covering the CIA's Torture program was revealed to the world.

At the time of writing this book, the "where" and the "'who" are still unclear and nothing more than informed speculation exists, but the full extent is now known of what the ubiquitous phrase "enhanced interrogation techniques" really means.

By the time a top secret report detailing the CIA's justification and defense of its interrogation programs during the early stages of the GWOT is published, the shocking impact of 9/11 may well have subsided, leaving the report as more of an historical document than a contemporary example of intelligence work.

As it stands today, there are those who feel that the release of the grim contents, spread across 6,700 pages, will be far more damaging to America's national security, and possibly endanger the lives of its citizens overseas, if published in their entirety. For make no mistake, the contents are, in the words of US Senator Dianne Feinstein, *"truly shocking."*

What we do know from the heavily censored report released in December 2014 is that at least 119 people were held for months and years in secret CIA overseas sites between 2002 and 2007 in conditions described as inhumane. We also know that many of these detainees were waterboarded, endured excessive sleep deprivation, mock executions and physical beatings, as well as sexually bizarre techniques.

The then chair of the Senate Select Committee on Intelligence, Democratic Senator Feinstein, writes in the foreword of the report summary that nothing, not even the September 11 attacks, could *"justify, temper, or excuse improper actions taken by individuals and organizations in the name of national security."*

Heralded as one of the most important US government documents ever released, the scale of the $40 million probe that went into producing the summary was unprecedented. Based on no less than 6 million CIA documents scanned and read from early 2009 to late 2012, the 6,700-page original report is still off limits. The redacted summary outlines in ghastly, meticulous detail exactly how America violated its own founding principles of freedom and democracy.

Graphic accounts, previously only suspected by lawyers and human rights groups, can now be viewed by outsiders and confirmed in black and white official government print for the first time. The contents revealed how the world's most famous spy agency, the CIA, allowed some of its employees to embark on bizarre practices like "rectal force feeding" on hardened al-Qaeda and Islamist suspects in the hope of extracting information to fight the GWOT. Until the publication of this report, these sorts of methods had been euphemistically described as EITs.

Some of the EITs appear not to have been approved and involved extreme stress positions and exposure to freezing cold temperatures designed to induce hypothermia, and involved the use of water hoses and ice baths.

The Senate committee said its original intention back in 2009 was to learn from and develop policies which would shape future detention and interrogation methods, according to Feinstein, who adds in her own summary: *"It is my sincere and deep hope that through the release of these Findings and Conclusions and Executive Summary that U.S. policy will never again allow for secret indefinite detention and the use of coercive interrogations."*[1]

The report is highly critical of the CIA but perhaps some context should be given before rushing to judge its contents; 9/11 provided the backdrop and was the largest- ever strike on homeland America in the country's history. Even though CIA Director George Tenet had warned the Senate Intelligence Committee in the summer of 2001 to brace itself for a "possible major terrorist event," nothing could possibly have prepared the American people or their government for the horrors that were about to unfold.

By around 8.48am on the morning of that fateful day, the speculation of "if, when and how" ended abruptly in New York City. Terrible images of the wreckage of a

---

1   Senator Dianne Feinstein, then Chairman of the Senate Select Committee on Intelligence, in her foreword to the official Senate report on the CIA's detention and interrogation program.

crashed passenger airliner contained within an inferno inside the burning frame of the World Trade Center towers in Lower Manhattan were broadcast live to the world. In Arlington, Virginia, the Pentagon was hit by another passenger airliner. A fourth plane was brought down by its passengers to prevent another building being struck. In total, 2996 people died, more than 6,000 others were injured and a nation was traumatized for years to come. The world had changed forever.

The climate of fear in the days, weeks, months and years to follow was palpable and is still in evidence today as hoax emails and terror alerts can affect entire state administrations.[2]

Stephen Kinzer, a senior fellow at the Watson Institute for International Studies at Brown University, wrote about the "United States of Fear and Panic" to describe the fragile condition of fellow Americans in an article in the Boston Globe.[3] He wrote:

"During the Cold War, Americans were told that we were liable to be incinerated by Soviet bombs at any moment. Ever since the Soviet Union had the bad manners to collapse a quarter-century ago, we have been suffering from enemy deprivation syndrome. Islamic terror has cured us.

"One recent survey suggests that half of all Americans now fear that they or a loved one will be victim of a terror attack. A mass shooting in San Bernardino, Calif. set off this latest wave of fear. It was the second act of apparently religion-inspired terror in the United States during 2015. Together they took a total of 19 lives. Also during 2015, about 30,000 Americans died in road crashes. Ten thousand were shot to death. More than 40 died in accidents involving toasters. Mass killings only stun us when they are connected to Islam or the Middle East."

If Kinzer's "enemy deprivation syndrome" existed, it was certainly brought to an abrupt end by the events of 9/11; that evening, US President George W Bush made a national TV address to assure the American people that he would do whatever was necessary to avoid another attack on US soil. Speaking to the theme of revenge, he said: *"The search is underway for those who were behind these evil acts. I have directed the full resources of our intelligence and law enforcement communities to*

---

2   California schools were closed for the day on December 15 2015 after a terror scare. Accessed at http://touch.latimes.com/#section/-1/article/p2p-85329505/.

3   Published on December 23 2015 and accessed at https://www.bostonglobe.com/opinion/2015/12/23/the-united-states-fear-and-panic/o3Dvdxl1nUw45Z2Lza9aLM/story.html.

find those responsible and to bring them to justice. We will make no distinction between the terrorists who committed these acts and those who harbor them."

While he did not insert any codicils or conditions into his speech, it is clear from the pages outlining CIA abuse and torture that the agency believed it had a free pass to do what it felt was necessary to keep America safe. The methods of torture, outlined in excruciating detail, could not have been applied in a vacuum, but instead relied upon the explicit legal and political support of the Bush Administration, which obviously felt that the response to the extreme and exceptional events of 9/11 needed a similar response.

We now know, for instance, that guns were held to the heads of some detainees, while others had their children or close family threatened even though they were clearly third-party innocents. Cutting through all of the euphemistic language adopted by CIA officials, Senator Feinstein called it as she saw it in the report's preface: *"Under any common meaning of the term, CIA detainees were tortured."*

However, among the 2,700 footnotes or the tens of thousands of words, there is not one mention of the whereabouts of the CIA's secret prisons; the roles played by foreign governments in the GWOT including Britain and other allies; or basic information about kidnaps, renditions and tortures or all of the identities of the 119 prisoners mentioned in the report.

The so-called CIA Torture Report has polarized world opinion by creating two camps: those who think "by any means necessary" was a justified payback for 9/11 and those who argue that torture is non-negotiable in any democracy.

As yet there have been no direct political or legal consequences following the publication, although the current ban on torture is based only on a directive[4] from President Obama and could be revoked by the next President in January 2017. Various Republican presidential hopefuls have already vowed to undo Obama's executive orders if elected.[5]

---

4   Obama signed EO 13491 in January 2009 to ban the CIA from holding detainees other than on a "short-term transitory basis" and to limit interrogation techniques to those included in the Army Field Manual.

5   Republican Donald Trump told a rally in Mesa, Arizona in January 2016 that he would undo Obama's executive orders on his first day in office. "The good thing about an executive order – I walk in, sign, I don't have to go through Congress," he said. Accessed at http://www. huffingtonpost.com/entry/donald-trump-executive-orders_5671c88ee4b0688701dbfb29.

It remains to be seen if those politically responsible for allowing the torture of detainees will ever have to justify their decisions in a court of law, although, as mentioned elsewhere in this book, some members of the Bush Administration are already selective about where they travel overseas.

Philip Zelikow, former executive director of the 9/11 commission and counselor to former US Secretary of State Condoleezza Rice, told Deutsche Welle (DW) in December 2014:

> *"I supported the release of the report. I have been aware of its contents for more than two years. The existing media coverage is doing a pretty good job of explaining the key takeaways from the executive summary of the report. It is not just a historical document. It reinforces the importance of managing secret operations in a way that can sustain public trust and the support of our friends and allies in other countries."*

However, Karima Bennoune, professor of international law at the University of California-Davis School of Law, gave a different perspective when she spoke to DW during the same interview. She said:

> *"What we have learned is that the CIA torture program was even worse than previously understood – in scope, in the nature of detainee treatment, among other points. The report's release is important, but is only a first step. The United States is a state party to the UN Convention against Torture, and alleged perpetrators of torture must be brought to justice. The US cannot publicly admit to torture, and then take no legal action. This is simply not an option. No justification of torture – including terrorism – is ever permitted. Indeed, torture and terrorism follow the same logic. We must continue to staunchly oppose both. Security proponents must not justify violations of human rights, and human rights advocates must not minimize the reality of the threat to human rights from terrorism."*

Stephen Walt, professor of international affairs at Harvard University, pointed the finger of blame directly at the Bush Administration, saying that even with the redactions and omissions the content was a damning indictment, adding:

> *"Not only do they [the Bush Administration] appear to have violated domestic and international law, but their reliance on torture produced bad rather than good intelligence. These revelations are not entirely new, but it is important to have them confirmed in such an authoritative fashion.*

"The report is also useful in showing just how far the United States strayed from its basic ideals. It also reminds us that it is very difficult to control agencies that operate secretly, and especially when a society is frightened. The only question that remains is whether anyone will actually be held accountable."

Certainly, in the eyes of many, details of the CIA program appear to have been harsher and far more secretive than previously known. More important, details about the effectiveness of EITs appear to have been exaggerated, to the dismay of the pro-torture lobby, which insists on the simple narrative that torture produces good intelligence which in turn saves lives.

Some former CIA agents and their supporters have accused Feinstein's committee of politicizing a sensitive issue and giving impetus to claims that the GWOT is unjust and barbaric.

One group, describing itself as composed of ex-CIA officials with "hundreds of years of combined service" dismissed the significance of the report, saying it was *"marred by errors of facts and interpretation and is completely at odds with the reality."* Their views went live on a website called CIA Saved Lives.[6]

The website, set up to rebut any criticism, insisted that the capture of senior al-Qaeda leaders, including Osama bin Laden, was brought about through the EIT program; however, according to members of the Senate select committee, no useful intelligence was obtained as a result of torture.

In the meantime, hundreds of memoranda have appeared on the CIA Saved Lives website showing that White House and congressional leaders were kept well aware of the scope of the secret program.

"The Justice Department and White House were involved from the very beginning of the interrogation program," the group said, to counter claims by the committee report that the CIA misled administration officials and lawmakers about the extent of the interrogations' brutality.

---

6   The website went live on the day the report was published; accessed at http://www.ciasavedlives.com/.

When news reached Guantanamo that the US President had issued an executive order[7] making torture illegal there was great excitement among the detainees, according to Shaker Aamer, but it was short lived. During an informal meeting at his home in London, he told me there was no regime change or change in procedures. The torture, as far as he was concerned, continued.

When the executive order was issued by Obama there was an ongoing hunger strike in operation; the US answer to break the prisoners' determination to continue it was the employment of force feeding.

Aamer says he regarded the method of force feeding as torture since most who at the time were resisting food were strapped down to a chair. Restrained by their feet, ankles, legs, hands, wrists, arms and head, a feeding tube would be inserted forcibly through the nasal passages, often causing bleeding.

Occasionally the tube would strike the lungs, and on occasions it would come through the mouth of the detainee. As an act of resistance, those with quick enough reactions would bring the medical procedure to an abrupt halt by grabbing the tube with their teeth.

Until medics could prise open the jaw of the detainee, the force feeding would come to a halt. I remember handling the feeding tubes during a visit to the medical facilities at GTMO and noted that they were much wider in circumference than the tubes which had been used in Britain to force feed suffragettes. The practice was banned in the Victorian era, as it was deemed barbaric.

The Army colonel to whom I spoke during the making of the documentary "Inside the Wire"[8] assured me that the tubes were used on humanitarian grounds and to preserve life, although some released detainees said the aggressive techniques were designed to break their spirit and resistance, and end the strikes.

While his account remains challenged by the US authorities, what is not in dispute is the poignant speech given by Republican Senator John McCain, in which he praises the decision to release the torture report. This military veteran, who was elected to the US House of Representatives from Arizona in 1982 and to

---

7   Executive Order 13491 – "Ensuring Lawful Interrogations," issued January 22 2009.
8   The author, with film-maker David Miller, visited Guantanamo Bay prison in 2008. The documentary *Inside the Wire* has won several international awards.

the Senate four years later, was also the Republican Party's nominee for President in the 2008 election. His testimony given on the Senate Floor ahead of the report's release was all the more powerful because, as a POW, he endured firsthand the experience of torture.

Speaking from knowledge few would dare to challenge, McCain broke away from the views of his Republican colleagues, and even rebuked some of them, to commend the report. Using his own traumatic experience in Vietnam, the chairman of the Senate Committee on Armed Services held the floor for 15 minutes with his powerful testimony.

Speaking about his time as a POW in Vietnam, he reasoned that torture fails to yield credible information and said: *"I know from personal experience that the abuse of prisoners will produce more bad than good intelligence. I know that victims of torture will offer intentionally misleading information if they think their captors will believe it. I know they will say whatever they think their torturers want them to say if they believe it will stop their suffering."* He added: *"The use of torture compromises that which most distinguishes us from our enemies, our belief that all people, even captured enemies, possess basic human rights."*

Although neither Shaker Aamer nor John McCain seemed to have been in possession of any intelligence which would be useful to their interrogators, there is the fascinating case of Johann "Johnny" Jebsen, which emerged recently from declassified documents from World War II.

Jebsen was an anti-Nazi German intelligence officer who was "turned" by British intelligence and given the code name Artist. He was kidnapped from Lisbon by the Germans shortly before the D-Day invasion after they injected him with a drug which knocked him unconscious for the rendition.

When he awoke, he found himself in the Gestapo headquarters in Berlin, where his interrogation began in May 1944; by then, the Gestapo employed many methods of torture, including the masterful use of electrodes, rubber nightsticks, genital vices, soldering irons and cold baths in which prisoners were plunged to the point of drowning—a method not dissimilar to waterboarding.

Members of the French Resistance were advised to try and resist torture and remain silent for 24 hours after their capture, whereas the Gestapo boasted they could squeeze information out of any person within 48 hours. In a real-life ticking time bomb situation, Jebsen's abduction caused British intelligence huge concern, as he was aware of the plans for D-Day.[9] With less than three weeks to go, Jebsen could have changed the course of the war if had he talked.

He was last seen being dragged from an interrogation session wearing a bloodstained shirt and with at least one of his fingernails torn off,[10] wrote author Ben Macintyre. After the attentions of the Gestapo, he was barely recognisable: *"His flesh and muscle had melted away, and his head looked enormous, sitting on top of his wasted neck and shoulders."*

Jebsen's capture threatened to derail the D-Day invasion; MI5 was forced to tell wartime Prime Minister Winston Churchill of his capture but by May 20 the Germans still were unaware of what was to come. How and why he managed to resist the interrogation sessions is not known, but it is proof positive that torture can not be relied upon even when the victim does have valuable intelligence.

It is not an exaggeration to say that Jebsen's silence changed the course of the war and saved tens of thousands of lives in the process. He was indeed what could be referred to as the original ticking time bomb but the Germans never knew it.

As Macintyre says in the final paragraph of his book, Jebsen *"resisted his Gestapo torturers to the end. Like many ordinary, flawed people, he did not know his own courage until war revealed it. Jebsen might easily have turned history into a disastrous direction to save his own skin, and he chose not to. Agent Artist was not a conventional D-Day hero, but he was a hero nonetheless."*

The ticking time bomb scenario is often cited by the pro-torture lobby as a reason to resort to inflicting pain in exchange for life-saving information; this subject is covered in more depth in the following chapter.

---

9   D-Day, or the Normandy Landings, was the largest seaborne invasion in history.

10   Macintyre, Ben: *Double Cross: The True Story of the D-Day Spies.* London, Bloomsbury, 2012, p. 297.

5
The Ticking Bomb Scenario

The concept of the much quoted ticking time bomb scenario, in which countless lives of innocents could be saved on the basis of intelligence extracted under torture, is often cited by the pro-torture lobby to justify the use of harsh interrogation techniques like those outlined in previous pages. However, the origins of the concept are not exclusive to the GWOT, as the scenario has been played out in the minds of philosophers, playwrights, authors, Hollywood scriptwriters and others involved in works of both fact and fiction.

Eminent theologians and philosophers have, over the centuries, wrestled with the challenges presented by the so-called "lesser of two evils" concept[1] famously popularised to a Second World War generation during a House of Commons speech by Sir Winston Churchill.

When Germany invaded the Soviet Union in June 1941, forcing Churchill into an alliance with the Soviets, he was taunted by a group of fellow parliamentarians, who knew him to despise communism and the Soviet Union. He retorted in his speech to their comments by declaring: *If Hitler were to invade Hell, I would at least make a favourable reference to the Devil in the House of Commons.*

The two evils concept is well known to theological scholars and academics familiar with the work of St Thomas Aquinas,[2] who reasoned in his Summa Theologica[3] that it is acceptable for a man to kill someone to save his own life but the attack could not be justified if it was carried out merely to kill the attacker. Aquinas concluded[4] that God gives permission to a victim to protect him/herself by killing the assailant in an unprovoked attack.

---

1   During World War II, the Western Allies justified their support for Russia's Communist leader Joseph Stalin under a lesser of two evils principle.

2   Thomas Aquinas (1225–1274): Italian Dominican priest, philosopher, theologian and patron of Catholic universities, colleges and schools.

3   Regarded as one of the classics of the history of philosophy and one of the most influential works of Western literature.

4   Aquinas, Thomas: *The Summa Theologica*. London, Burns Oates & Washbourne Ltd., May 1911, Question: 2a2ae, 64.7. For a biography, see: Chesterton, GK: *St Thomas Aquinas*. London, Hodder and Stoughton, 1943.

His principle of the "lesser of the two evils," also referred to by Aquinas as the "double effect"[5] on issues of self defence, is applicable today with regard to the waging of modern warfare; it is arguably relevant to the question of torture being used as a weapon to save lives. However, the ethical dilemmas taken up by Aquinas in the 13th century had already challenged the minds of other great thinkers and philosophers, including Aristotle,[6] who revealed in his best known work, the Nichomachean Ethics, in 350 BCE: "*[To] do this to the right person, to the right extent, at the right time, with the right motive, and in the right way, that is not for every one nor is it easy; wherefore goodness is both rare and laudable and noble.*"

The 20th century philosopher, novelist and playwright Jean-Paul Sartre[7] explored the hypothetical subject of saving many lives by sacrificing one in his 1940s play "Les Mains Sales",[8] which was about the assassination of a leading politician; however, the question posed in the plot is whether the killer's motivations were political or personal. Thus, the play's main theme does not focus on who did it, but why. The conclusion appears to justify the killing on the basis that since politics is such a dirty business, no one taking part can hope to keep either hands or conscience clean.

It was an ethical dilemma which gripped the Parisian theatre class, but the issue probably first came into the wider public's consciousness during the 1960s through the French best-seller "Les Centurions"[9] written by French journalist Jean Pierre Lucien Osty, using the nom de plume Jean Lartéguy. He had previously done military service with the Free French Forces (FFF),[10] when he became a highly decorated soldier. He then became a war correspondent, reporting from many conflict areas, including Azerbaijan, Korea, Palestine, Indochina, Algeria and Vietnam. It was his book "Les Centurions", however, that defined him as a writer who won acclaim for his ability to translate personal experiences as a soldier on to the pages of his novels through graphic details.

---

5   Aquinas, Thomas: *The Summa Theologica*. Question: 2a2ae, 64.7.

6   See also Aristotle: *Nicomachean Ethics*, Hackett Publishing Company, 2006. For a biography, see: Barnes, Jonathan: The Cambridge Companion to Aristotle, 1995.

7   Regarded as the father of Existentialist philosophy, whose writings set the tone for intellectual life in the decade immediately following the Second World War.

8   *Les Mains Sales*, translated as Dirty Hands, was first performed as a political drama in Paris in 1948. It is set in the fictional country of Illyria between 1943–1945.

9   Lartéguy, Jean: *The Centurions*. Presses de la Cite, 1960. The book sold more than 420,000 copies.

10   In 1940, General Charles de Gaulle launched the Forces Françaises Libres from London. More than 100,000 FFF fought in the Anglo-American campaign in Italy in 1943 and, by the time of the Allied invasion of Normandy in June 1944, their ranks had swelled to more than 300,000 regular troops.

In "Les Centurions", he portrays the French troops as latter-day Roman centurions holding the line against the barbarians, exactly as their Roman ancestors had done along Hadrian's Wall.[11] Lartéguy's books extolled the self-sacrifice of commando soldiers who were unappreciated or even reviled back home, but were the bulwark separating anarchy and order. The novel opens in May 1954 with the defeat of the French army at Dien Bien Phu.[12] The Vietnamese victors then march their French prisoners into communist re-education camps; during their time in captivity, the French paratroop officers who survive the ordeal to be repatriated bond together and try to utilise communist *"revolutionary war"* tactics to win their next conflict in Algeria.

The plot centres on a ticking time bomb scenario in which torture is used to force critical information from a female Arab dissident to learn the location of bombs planted throughout the city of Algiers and thus save many lives.

The story gripped the imagination of the French public, which turned the book into a bestseller; decades later, it would have a similar impact on the other side of the Atlantic, and it is now evident that the French military experience in Algeria provided a major influence for a whole new generation of US military strategists who could identify with similar insurgency challenges presented by the wars in Afghanistan and Iraq.

This influence is illustrated by the fact that US General David Petraeus,[13] who oversaw the writing of a new US field manual for counter-insurgency[14] in 2006, makes no secret of the fact that he drew heavily on the Algerian war era and includes a direct reference to it in his opening foreword. In the history of Petraeus' association with counter-insurgency (COIN) campaigns and his personal supervision in the compiling of FM 3-24, the Algerian war provided a solid influence, along with those officers who distinguished themselves in the French military by defining COIN in their own distinct way.

---

11   A defensive fortification built during the rule of Emperor Hadrian in Roman Britain. For more information, see: Birley, Anthony R: *Hadrian: The Restless Emperor*. Routledge Publishing, 1997.

12   A town in northwest Vietnam near the Laotian border. The French military base there fell to Vietminh troops on May 7 1954, after a 56-day siege, leading to the end of France's involvement in Indochina.

13   David Petraeus achieved the rank of four-star general in 2007. He served for more than 37 years in the US Army and held the position of Commander, U.S. Army Combined Arms Center when he oversaw the publication of the new manual. On Petraeus, see Broadwell, Paula: *All In*. Penguin, 2012.

14   *US Army Field Manual 3-24. Counterinsurgency*. Marine Corps Warfighting Publication. No 3-33.5. Washington, 2006.

Acknowledging that it had been 20 years since the US Army had published a field manual devoted exclusively to COIN, Petraeus wrote:

> *"The Army and Marine Corps recognize that every insurgency is contextual and presents its own set of challenges. You cannot fight former Saddamists and Islamic extremists the same way you would have fought the Viet Cong, Moros, or Tupamaros; the application of principles and fundamentals to deal with each varies considerably. Nonetheless, all insurgencies, even today's highly adaptable strains, remain wars amongst the people. They use variations of standard themes and adhere to elements of a recognizable revolutionary campaign plan. This manual therefore addresses the common characteristics of insurgencies. It strives to provide those conducting counterinsurgency campaigns with a solid foundation for understanding and addressing specific insurgencies."*

French Lieutenant Colonel David Galula[15] also is quoted and referenced in FM 3-24 as being only one of three individuals selected for a special mention in the preface's acknowledgement's section.[16] One of his books is cited under the title "The Classics" in the manual's bibliography.[17]

US strategists also frequently quote another favourite of that era, Colonel Roger Trinquier.[18] As a veteran of the Algerian war, he was critical of the French military's slow adaptation of new tactics. In his book on modern warfare, Trinquier unashamedly advocated torture as a means of extracting vital information from the enemy,[19] whereas the US counter-insurgency manual explicitly prohibits its

---

15   A French military officer (1919–1967) influential in developing the theory and practice of counter-insurgency warfare. During the Algerian war, he distinguished himself by applying personal tactics in counterinsurgency to his sector near Tigzirt, effectively eliminating the nationalist insurgency and earning accelerated promotion from captain. In 1958, Galula was transferred to the Headquarters of National Defence in Paris. He resigned his commission in 1962 to study in the United States, where he obtained a position of research associate at the Center for International Affairs of Harvard University.

16   *US Army Field Manual 3-24. Counterinsurgency*. Marine Corps Warfighting Publication. No. 3-33.5. Washington. Preface viii Acknowledgements; *Counterinsurgency Warfare: Theory and Practice*, David Galula. Frederick A. Praeger, Inc., 1964. Reproduced Westport CT, Greenwood Publishing Group, Inc., December 2006.

17   Galula, David: *Counterinsurgency Warfare: Theory and Practice*. London, Praeger, 1964, p. 45.

18   A French Army officer during World War II, the First Indochina War and the Algerian war, serving mainly in airborne and special forces units. He was also a counter-insurgency theorist and authored a book on the subject.

19   Trinquier, Roger: *Modern Warfare: A French View of Counterinsurgency*. Connecticut, Praeger Security International, 2006.

use,[20] saying the practice plays into the hands of insurgents and undermines America's "moral legitimacy."

Trinquier's fourth chapter, on terrorism, states that terrorists should be treated outside of the rules of war until after interrogation. His criteria for torture was that the terrorist was to be asked only questions related to his group and that the torture must stop once the information is obtained, with the terrorist then receiving the same treatment as any other POW. Laying out his justification for operating outside Hague and Geneva Conventions, he wrote:[21]

> *"The terrorist operates within a familiar legal framework, while avoiding the ordinary risks taken by the common criminal, let alone by soldiers on the field of battle, or even by partisans facing regular troops ... Not only does he carry on warfare without uniform, but he attacks, far from a field of battle, only unarmed civilians who are incapable of defending themselves and who are normally protected under the rules of warfare ... he runs practically no risk – neither that of retaliation by his victims nor that of having to appear before a court of justice ... he must be made to realize that, when he is captured, he can not be treated as an ordinary criminal, nor like a prisoner taken on a battlefield."*

In their various accounts, he and his colleagues wrote that they regarded their captives as terrorists who, in their view, could be treated outside of the law. Galula even makes a sneering reference to the reliance on or use of a legal process in a heading called "Direct Action Against the Insurgent" in his book on COIN warfare. He wrote:[22]

> *"The arrested insurgent can count almost automatically on some support from the legitimate opposition parties and groups. Referred to the courts, he will take refuge in chicanery and exploit to the utmost every advantage provided by the existing laws. Worse yet, the trial itself will serve as a sounding board for his cause."*

Not one of Galula's or Trinquier's books studied for this work give any legal basis or standing to justify the use of torture on insurgents; while POWs are protected by the Geneva Conventions, these authors did not acknowledge or grant such a

---

20   *US Army Field Manual 3-24. Counterinsurgency*. Marine Corps Warfighting Publication. No. 3-33.5. Washington. "Appendix D3, Legal Considerations – The Law of War" (Point 3): Soldiers and Marines Do Not Kill or Torture Enemy Prisoners of War.

21   Trinquier: *Modern Warfare*, p. 16–18.

22   Galula: *Counterinsurgency Warfare*, p. 45.

status to those swept up in the Algerian war. One can only conclude that this was a blatant disregard for basic human rights as outlined in the conventions – and it appears to have been emulated decades later by the Bush Administration in reaction to 9/11.

International humanitarian law is composed of two main branches; the law of The Hague and the law of Geneva. The former regulates the means and methods of warfare and governs the actual conduct of hostilities, including issues such as the selection of targets and weapons permissible for use in a conflict. The law of Geneva, on the other hand, is codified within the four conventions adopted in 1949 for the protection of civilians, the wounded and prisoners of war, as outlined in Chapter 2 of this work, which discusses the definitions of torture in great detail.

Significantly, under "Leadership and Ethics for Counterinsurgency" the COIN manual, drawing on the experiences and legacy of the Algerian war, states quite clearly:[23]

"During the Algerian war of independence between 1954 and 1962, French leaders decided to permit torture against suspected insurgents. Though they were aware that it was against the law and morality of war, they argued that—

• *This was a new form of war and these rules did not apply.*

• *The threat the enemy represented, communism, was a great evil that justified extraordinary means.*

• *The application of torture against insurgents was measured and non-gratuitous.*

This official condoning of torture on the part of French Army leadership had several negative consequences. It empowered the moral legitimacy of the opposition, undermined the French moral legitimacy, and caused internal fragmentation among serving officers that led to an unsuccessful coup attempt in 1962. In the end, failure to comply with moral and legal restrictions against torture severely undermined French efforts and contributed to their loss despite several significant military victories.

---

23   *US Army Field Manual 3-24. Counterinsurgency.* Marine Corps Warfighting Publication. No. 3-33.5. Washington. *Leadership and Ethics for Counterinsurgency.*

Illegal and immoral activities made the counterinsurgents extremely vulnerable to enemy propaganda inside Algeria among the Muslim population, as well as in the United Nations and the French media. These actions also degraded the ethical climate throughout the French Army. France eventually recognized Algerian independence in July 1963."

This critical observation tends to conflict directly with the decision-making process in the Bush Administration, which led directly to the development and authorisation of the EITs for so-called enemy combatants; it also seemingly makes clear exactly where Petraeus and the US Army stood on the issue of torture. Otherwise, one assumes, he would not have been so direct in his condemnation of how destructive the practice of torture was during the Algerian campaign.

Could it be that as a military officer, Petraeus felt he was able to distance himself from the political decision making of the Bush Administration, thereby invoking the conclusion of Sartre's "Les Mains Sales", which projects politics as the real dirty business in which it is the politicians who have dirty hands? It is interesting to note that Petraeus, while in uniform, was obviously comfortable with condemning the Algerian methods of torture.

However, when the subject of torture was raised during his 2011 confirmation hearing to become head of the CIA, it seems that the former general adopted a more political stance, abandoning his opposition to EIT; instead, when he was asked about his position on torture, he parroted the now familiar ticking bomb scenario, which could present a "special situation." According to this opinion piece[24] in the Washington Post, Petraeus said:

"... torture might be justified if you have a 'special situation' where an "individual in your hands who you know has placed a nuclear device under the Empire State Building. It goes off in 30 minutes, he has the codes to turn it off." [Then he urged legislators to consider crafting such an exception into the law.] "I think that is a special case. I think there should be discussion of that by policymakers and by Congress. I think that it should be thought out ahead of time. There should be a process if indeed there is going to be something more than, again, the normal techniques employed in such a case. And again, I – I would certainly submit that that would be very helpful if that kind of debate could be held and if some resolution could be made as to what should be done in a case like that so that it is worked out ahead of time, rather than under an extraordinary sense of pressure in such a situation."

---

24   Serwer, Adam: "Did General Petraeus Change His Position on Torture?" *Washington Post*, Opinion Column, June 24 2011.

Later, in an exchange with Senator John McCain, Petraeus said that he believed it should be *"a nuclear football kind of procedure where … there is an authorization, but it has to come from the top … this can't be something where we are forcing low-level individuals to have to make a choice under enormous duress."*

Despite Petraeus' seemingly conflicting views on torture, perhaps the fact that Trinquier's work is also credited in the US Army US Army Field Manual 3-24 bibliography[25] could be viewed as a sign that Petraeus may have held a certain admiration for the methodology of COIN as carried out by the French in Algeria. A further clue was revealed the following year in a defensive email to a journalist at the news agency Agence France-Presse (AFP), when Petraeus wrote[26] that both Trinquier and Galula:

"Captured with considerable nuance the conduct of counter-insurgency operations of that day, and a good bit of the way those operations were conducted remains instructive and relevant."

It would be easy to conclude that Petraeus, while identifying with both of these French officers and their experiences in COIN, shows his diplomatic side through a careful choice of words by saying that some – not all – of their methods are relevant today, thereby promoting their presence in the US Army US Army Field Manual 3-24 without giving 100 percent endorsement of their unorthodox methods of interrogation techniques and handling of insurgents.

It is clear that Petraeus and other soldiers appeared to find kindred spirits in these French military men, even though the former were obviously uncomfortable with the methods commonly deployed in that era. Could it be that the US military's unease was caused by the frank and matter-of-fact manner in which some senior French military officers openly admitted that torture was carried out in Algeria?

The Lartéguy novel, equally forthright, ends with the French centurions fighting the Battle of Algiers with propaganda, torture, terror and any tactic that comes to hand to win so that the last remnants of their empire could survive.

---

25   Trinquier: *Modern Warfare.*

26   His email was sent to AFP agency in response to a request for a comment for an article published on March 15 2012 marking the 50th anniversary of the French-Algerian war. Dispatched to media customers by the agency, it was entitled "Algeria conflict shapes US military strategy." By this time, Petraeus was the Director of the CIA.

After its success in France, the book went on to sell millions of copies around the world and was later turned into the movie "The Lost Command."[27] It is also credited with having inspired in recent years a number of television programmes, including the hugely popular "24"[28] starring Kiefer Sutherland, whose character is Counter Terrorist Unit (CTU) agent Jack Bauer. The success of this book and television programme is significant, as it shows the potential for persuading people that torture is a necessary evil as long as it is presented to a patriotic public as a matter of life and death.

Lartéguy's ticking bomb scenario may have been a work of fiction; for many, however, its contents are regarded as more than mere make believe and the stuff of Hollywood plots. As America became more entrenched in the Vietnam War, his book was studied by American officers and Special Forces soldiers. "Les Centurions" then regained currency once more with the onset of 9/11, the GWOT and the insurgency phase of the Iraq War. Since then, it and other titles related to the Algerian war have become almost required reading for those working on COIN.[29]

Those who have heaped critical acclaim on the book, describing it as such an accurate piece of fiction about counter-insurgency and terrorism that military professionals should be required to read it, include Petraeus, who praised its contents as a way to understand terrorism and insurgency in the GWOT.[30] Due to its very accurate portrayal of events that occurred in real life, combined with a psychologically challenging plot, Les Centurions and books by Galula[31] have also become required reading for students and historians of COIN and the Algerian war.[32]

---

27   "Lost Command," directed by Mark Robson, was first shown in 1966.

28   Premiering on November 6 2001, "24" was syndicated worldwide. The show spanned 192 episodes over eight seasons.

29   US Army & Marine Counterinsurgency Center PowerPoint presentation of January 8 2009, "COIN Training Resources & Strategies" names several books, including *Modern Warfare* by Roger Trinquier and *Counterinsurgency Warfare, Theory & Practice* by David Galula as "Recommended COIN Books."

30   Raday, Sophia: "David Petraeus Wants this French Novel Back in Print!" Slate online magazine, January 27 2011, accessed at http://www.slate.com/id/2282462/.

31   French COIN expert David Galula moved to the US, where he completed *Pacification in Algeria, 1956–1958* and *Counterinsurgency Warfare: Theory and Practice* during fellowships at the RAND Corporation and Harvard University, respectively. The latter volume is now part of the US Army Command and General Staff College curriculum.

32   The conflict between France and Algeria from 1954 to 1962 led to Algeria gaining its independence from France. It was characterised by guerrilla warfare, terrorism against civilians and the use of torture on both sides.

In 2011 US author Sophia Raday[33] wrote an in-depth analysis revealing plans to have "Les Centurions" republished because of the revival in interest over its contents. In revisiting the contents, she draws real-life parallels with the plots and characters, writing that the novel had once again become relevant, especially in the incendiary political climate which produced the GWOT. Among those she name checks in her article is the famous French military officer Lieutenant General (Général de corps d'armée) Marcel Bigeard,[34] who fought in World War II, Indochina and Algeria. As one of the commanders in the Battle of Dien Bien Phu, he is thought by many to have been a dominating influence on French thinking regarding "unconventional" warfare. She also makes reference to and comparisons with controversial US General Stanley McChrystal,[35] who upset the Obama Administration with revelations and criticisms he made in a frank article published in a Rolling Stone profile;[36] many believed it ultimately ended his career in uniform.

Raday wrote:

"The chapters set in Algeria closely parallel Petraeus' experiences in Iraq. In 2005, as it became patently obvious that we were losing the war, Petraeus advocated a new approach — one of counter-insurgency or COIN, which differs from conventional war doctrine in that it emphasizes the essentially political (as opposed to military) character of insurrection ... FM 3-24 established Petraeus as a 'scholar-general,' and shifted our military's priorities from brief displays of massive firepower to patience and adaptability, advocating, in particular, the quick incorporation of lessons from the field. Raspeguy [see note 34] would cheer.

"The similarities between The Centurions and modern-day COIN are no accident. Not only is Petraeus known to regularly re-read portions of the book, he also was something of a disciple of Marcel Bigeard ... Petraeus corresponded with Bigeard for three decades, and keeps an inscribed photo of the French general on his desk ... Larteguy has a knack for setting up psychologically intense situations that both demonstrate military ideals (loyalty, leading from the front, courage) as well as

---

33   Sophia Raday is a writer and the author of *Love in Condition Yellow: A Memoir of an Unlikely Marriage*, which draws on her experience as the wife of a soldier deployed in Iraq in 2007.

34   The character of Pierre-Noel Raspeguy in Les Centurions by Lartéguy is believed to be modelled largely on Marcel Bigeard.

35   Stanley McChrystal is a retired four-star general. His last assignment was Commander, International Security Assistance Force (ISAF) and Commander, US Forces Afghanistan (USFOR-A).

36   Hastings, Michael: "The Runaway General," *Rolling Stone*, July 8–22 2010, p. 1108–1109. Accessed at http://www.rollingstone.com/politics/news/the-runaway-general-20100622#ixzz1pZeQkdyU.

the anguish of war. He is credited, for instance, with first using the 'ticking bomb scenario.' Raspeguy and company capture a rebel leader who knows the location of 15 bombs set to go off in various European shops in Algiers in exactly 24 hours, and they must, naturally, extract this information in time. Many details from this scene, including a prominently featured clock showing elapsed time, were used repeatedly in the TV drama 24. But in 24, the 'ticking bomb scenario' is used to heighten dramatic tension, and some would say, as a justification for doing 'whatever it takes' to get terrorists to talk."

Warming to the theme, Raday also references the real personalities by contrasting and comparing them to the characters in Lartéguy's novel who occasionally brush with their superiors and political masters.

"Gen. Petraeus seems to have avoided such extreme disaffection. But Gen. Stanley McChrystal, former commander of the U.S. forces in Afghanistan, better fits the Larteguyan mold. It's clear that McChrystal has read The Centurions and has felt the special soldierly bond that Larteguy describes. In one of his last major interviews, McChrystal told the Atlantic: 'We in JSOC [Joint Special Operations Command] had this sense of ... mission, passion ... I don't know what you call it. The insurgents had a real cause, and we had a counter-cause. We had a level of unit cohesion just like in The Centurions.'"

It thus becomes obvious how the so-called ticking bomb scenario came to seep into the popular consciousness of those who read "Les Centurions" or the millions more who watched the fictional TV series it went on to inspire in later decades, especially after 9/11. The plot may have come from the pages of fiction but it was indeed based on real experiences through the eyes of Lartéguy; such was the authenticity of his writings and observations that his work influenced not only popular culture but subsequent generations of soldiers, lawyers, politicians and other major opinion makers.

Galula's influence in particular was singled out at the Strategic Studies Institute (SSI) in a 73-page published report authored by Anne Marlowe[37] in celebration of his life. She wrote:

"When Galula lived in the United States off and on between 1960 and 1963, he participated in the first American awakening to COIN under the auspices of President

---

37   Anne Marlowe is a writer who has spoken on Afghanistan to the US Army, the US Army War College, the US State Department and college students.

John Kennedy. But the voluminous literature produced during this period – not to mention that of guerre revolutionaire – had been forgotten by all but a few military historians by the publication in December 2006 of the U.S. Army US Army Field Manual 3-24, Counterinsurgency. So Galula's eventual fame belongs to the COIN fever of our time, not his own."[38]

Although perhaps only military strategists, historians, philosophers and other academics would be familiar with the controversial work of Galula, Trinquier and Bigeard, their legacy already has been subliminally embedded in the psyche of the masses – bear in mind the "24" TV series was watched by millions around the globe[39] – making it relatively easy for adherents of torture to use their scenario to gain popular support for their arguments.

Ordinary members of the public began to recognise the scenario but, because of Hollywood-style spin and glamour, they already were sold on the concept that torture of a terror suspect would be permissible to save thousands of lives.

According to academic Alfred W McCoy,[40] it became difficult for many Americans to distinguish between fact and fiction,[41] and he accused US President of George W Bush of capitalising on this scenario, even apportioning blame to Bush for deliberately blurring the lines between fantasy and reality.

He illustrated this in a hugely critical article he wrote for The Progressive[42] in 2006, recounting a live TV appearance given by Bush with relatives of those who died in 9/11 just days before its fifth anniversary. He likened the press conference in the East Room of the White House to a scene from "24", writing:

"With clipped, secret-agent diction reminiscent of the show's Emmy Award-winning star, Kiefer Sutherland, Bush said he was transferring fourteen top Al-Qaeda captives … to Guantánamo Bay. At once both repudiating and legitimating past abuses, Bush

---

38   Marlowe, Anne: *David Galula: His Life and Intellectual Context*. Series: SSI Books. Carlisle, Strategic Studies Institute of the US Army War College (SSI), August 2010.

39   Viewers' ratings in the US alone ranked between 8.6 and 13.78 million during its 10-year run.

40   JRW Smail Professor of History at the University of Wisconsin-Madison and author of *A Question of Torture: CIA Interrogation, from the Cold War to the War on Terror.*

41   McCoy, Alfred W: "The Myth of the Ticking Time Bomb." *The Progressive*, October 2006, p. 20–24.

42   *The Progressive* is a monthly left-wing magazine of investigative reporting, political commentary, cultural coverage and activism.

denied that he had ever authorized 'torture.' Simultaneously, he defended the CIA's effort to coerce 'vital information' from these 'dangerous' captives with what the President called an 'alternative set of procedures'—a euphemism transparent to any viewer of 24 ... Bush told his national television audience a thrilling tale of covert action derring-do almost plucked from the pages of a script for 24."

McCoy deliberately suspends belief in Bush's unsubstantiated claims that plots involving the use of anthrax, terror attacks and more airline hijackings had been thwarted because of "specific methods used in these CIA interrogations."

But what if Professor McCoy and the many other critics[43] of the ticking bomb theory are wrong, and torture is a necessary and effective weapon in the GWOT and can help save the lives of innocents?

It is a question that has focused the mind of Harvard Law School's Professor Alan Dershowitz for more than a decade. He is convinced of the authenticity of the ticking bomb scenario regardless of its origins and despite what the anti-torture lobby says. He, of all of those on the opposing side, must have been delighted when Petraeus not only appeared to change his view at his CIA confirmation hearing before the US Senate Select Committee on Intelligence, but appeared to call[44] for official permission to torture; this testimony must have boosted morale in the camp of Dershowitz and his allies.

A cynic might say that Petraeus was simply covering his own back as the future head of the CIA by urging lawmakers to create protective legislation allowing for the use of EITs; as mentioned previously, he also warned: *"... but it has to come from the top ... this can't be something where we are forcing low-level individuals to have to make a choice under enormous duress."*

This call by Petraeus could be regarded as an official endorsement of the beliefs of Dershowitz, who first asked the question: Should the Ticking Bomb Terrorist

---

43   Published critics sourced for this document include Bob Brecher, the author of *Torture and the Ticking Bomb*; Jennifer K Harbury, author of *Truth, Torture and the American Way*; Jane Mayer, author of *The Dark Side*; Karen J Greenberg, co-editor of *The Torture Papers: The Road to Abu Ghraib*; and David Cole author of *The Torture Memos* – see the Bibliography for full references.

44   Minutes from the Statement of Record, US Senate Select Committee on Intelligence; Confirmation Hearing for General David H. Petraeus. June 23 2011.

be Tortured?[45] in 2002. He devotes an entire chapter to the subject in his book *Why Terrorism Works*; again, like so many advocates of the use of torture, his point of reference is 9/11.

Dershowitz writes:[46]

> *"Before September 11, 2001, no one thought the issue of torture would ever re-emerge as a topic of serious debate in this country. Yet shortly after that watershed event, FBI agents began to leak stories suggesting that they might have to resort to torture to get to some detainees, who were suspected of complicity in al-Qaeda terrorism, to provide information necessary to prevent a recurrence."*

Dershowitz reveals himself to be more of a pragmatist than a supporter of torture, and even condemns its use, but describes it as a "necessary evil" that "many nations routinely practice." It is obvious he is continually frustrated by the "don't ask, don't tell" policy as outlined by former CIA counterintelligence head Vincent Cannistraro[47] in a US newspaper article.

"Many nations that routinely practice the most brutal forms of torture are signatories to this convention, but they hypocritically ignore it," Dershowitz wrote in his ticking bomb chapter. Surely this begs the question of why is he regarded as a cheerleader for torture if he is against its use?

To be fair, the thrust of his argument is that he wants to legalise torture, stating it is wrong for the US Government to ignore the reality that torture is being practised under certain circumstances and should, therefore, make it legal and above board. Morals are not an issue in his argument which focuses purely on the legality of torture and operating within the confines of the law. Perhaps the most significant passage in the fourth chapter devoted to the ticking bomb scenario is the unveiling for the first time of his controversial concept of a *"torture warrant"* that would give interrogators a legal cover to employ harsh interrogation techniques without fear of prosecution further down the line.

---

45   Dershowitz, Alan M: *Why Terrorism Works: Understanding the Threat, Responding to the Challenge.* New Haven and London, Yale University Press, 2002.

46   Dershowitz: *Why Terrorism Works*

47   Drogin, Bob and Miller, Greg: "Spy Agencies Facing Questions of Tactics." *Los Angeles Times*, News Section. October 28 2001.

Perhaps it was this concept to which Petraeus alluded when he asked the US Select Committee on Intelligence to push this idea for legislation *"but it has to come from the top."*

Outlining his case for the implementation of a torture warrant in this passage, Dershowitz refers to a lecture he gave to some Israeli students:[48]

> *"I presented the following challenge to my Israeli audience: If the reason you permit non-lethal torture is based on the ticking bomb case, why not limit it exclusively to that compelling but rare situation? Moreover, if you believe that non-lethal torture is justifiable in the ticking bomb case, why not require advance judicial approval – 'a torture warrant'? That was the origin of a controversial proposal that has received much attention, largely critical, from the media. Its goal was, and remains, to reduce the use of torture to the smallest amount and degree possible, while creating public accountability for its rare use. I saw it not as a compromise with civil liberties but rather as an effort to maximize civil liberties in the face of a realistic likelihood that torture would, in fact, take place below the radar screen of accountability."*

Far from driving the practice of torture further underground, Dershowitz insists that his torture warrants would promote more transparency and prevent law-breaking, from lowly privates right up to the Commander in Chief (CINC). He explains as follows:[49]

> *"In a democracy governed by the rule of law, we should never want our soldiers or our President to take any action that we deem wrong or illegal ... No legal system operating under the rule of law should ever tolerate an 'off-the-books' approach to necessity ... The road to tyranny has always been paved with claims of necessity made by those responsible for the security of our nation."*

It is clear why Dershowitz's views hold so much influence and authority in the US, where he is regarded in some quarters as one of the best criminal defence and civil liberties lawyers.[50] However, his brutally frank opinions have also earned

---

48   Dershowitz, Alan M: *Why Terrorism Works*, p. 141.
49   Dershowitz: *Why Terrorism Works*, p. 152.
50   Beach, Bennett H and Yang, John E: "The Lawyer of Last Resort," *Time Magazine*, May 17 1982. In addition to including him on the cover story on the "50 Faces for the Future," Time also referred to him as *"the top lawyer of last resort in the country – a sort of judicial St. Jude."*

him a large number of critics from the academic and legal worlds, who have lined up to dismiss his ticking bomb arguments.

One of his most fierce critics is Bob Brecher, a Reader in Moral Philosophy at the University of Sussex in Brighton in the UK and the Director of its Centre for Applied Philosophy, Politics and Ethics. His book "Torture and the Ticking Bomb"[51] attempts to deconstruct the Dershowitz argument and launches into a personal attack on the first page of the preface as follows:

> *"It is because the general public is taking these academics seriously that there is an urgent need to expose how spurious their ideologically driven arguments are. The 'respectability' they confer on the argument that so-called ticking bombs justify torture, and that it had therefore better be regulated, needs to be countered ... The 'intellectual respectability' conferred by the academy is essential for that enterprise. Thus, since Alan Dershowitz's carefully constructed proposal to introduce torture warrants is both the most prominent and the most sophisticated of today's attempts to make torture respectable, it is his proposal we need to focus on."*

The thrust of the counter argument submitted by Brecher will feature elsewhere in this book, but since this section's focus is on the ticking bomb scenario it is worth seeking other informed opinions, such as that of another senior American academic, Dr Gabriel Palmer-Fernandez[52] who, having reviewed Brecher's book, described it in this way:

> *"... the most powerful and comprehensive challenge available to a piece of intellectual fraud having wide commerce today – that under some hypothetical situation the infliction of pain to break another's will is morally justifiable. The ticking bomb, in Brecher's analysis, is a fantasy that hardly yields grounds sufficient for the employment of interrogational torture. Here the philosopher's role towards that fantasy is quite clear: debunkify it!"*

Author Jennifer K. Harbury[53] also sets aside some editorial space for the ticking bomb and Dershowitz in her book "Truth, Torture, and the American Way" in which she concludes that torture does not work and therefore the ticking bomb would prove

---

51   Brecher, Bob: *Torture and the Ticking Bomb*, London, Blackwell Publishing, 2007.
52   Director of the Dr James Dale Ethics Center and a member of the faculty department of Philosophy and Religious Studies at Youngstown State University, Ohio.
53   Human rights activist and lead member of Stop Torture Permanently (STOP).

useless. She further adds:[54]*"Any police officer who literally saved the world by torturing an individual prisoner is a very unlikely candidate for prosecution ... Alan Dershowitz has argued that since torture will be used whether we like it or not, strict legal standards should be established to limit its use."*

Her hypothetical example is rather poignant and possibly unfortunate, because in Germany senior police did have to confront a time-sensitive crime in 2002, when the 11-year-old son of a wealthy family was kidnapped. Faced with a real ticking clock, police resorted to threats to torture the kidnap suspect in a desperate bid to find the boy.[55] The suspect taunted his interrogators that the child would starve to death and refused to disclose his victim's location until officers resorted to issuing threats of torture. One even threatened to have him *"raped"* by a predatory inmate. The kidnapper broke down, admitted that he had killed the child and led interrogators to the body.

As the details of the interrogation emerged, German legal experts began debating whether the administration of non-lethal torture would have been appropriate – morally and legally – under those compelling circumstances. They got their answer in August 2011 when a judge ordered nearly €3,000 in compensation be paid to Magnus Gäfgen, the child killer.[56]

The state court made the award on the grounds that Gäfgen's "human dignity" had been impinged upon during an interrogation by police, who thought his victim was still alive. Germany's Interior Minister Otto Schily defended the decision and said:[57] *"If we begin to relativize the ban on torture then we are putting ourselves back in the darkest Middle Ages and risk putting all of our values into question."*

However, when asked whether the ban on torture was absolute and should apply even when the life of a child might be at stake, Mr. Schily responded: *"The police official in Frankfurt did not have any bad intentions when he made his threat. He was acting out of concern for the child, and that is honorable."*

---

54   Harbury, Jennifer, K: *Truth, Torture, and the American Way.* Boston, Beacon Press, 2005.

55   The murder, involving a member of one of Germany's oldest and best-known families, obsessed the media for weeks. In the months leading up to the trial, however, it was not so much the murder itself but the police resort to the threat of torture that aroused intense debate.

56   Ref: German Internet news site "Deutsche Welle."

57   Bernstein, Richard: "Kidnapping Has Germans Debating Police Torture," *New York Times,* April 10 2003, p. 2.

The judgement and ruling was significant because the German case reached into the heart of the philosophical debate that all humans and their dignities are equal. The conclusion reached by the German judiciary clashes directly with the view presented by Thomas Aquinas in his "Summa Theologica" that an unprovoked attacker forfeits his dignity and can therefore be killed. In other words, using the Aquinas argument, the torture by the police chief would have been admissible.

Although biblical laws forbid murder, Aquinas supported what he regarded as the right of a human being to protect and defend himself. In a wider context it therefore could be argued that the same challenges are faced by soldiers of war, who are sometimes faced with a stark choice of kill or be killed.

The German court's ruling made clear that the responsibility for actions must be borne by the individual and not by a group or organization, such as the police force in this particular case. In other words, the court was rejecting the idea of a "volonté generale" ("General Will") as promoted by philosopher Jean-Jacques Rousseau[58] who argued, according to his followers, that the role of an organization or a state should be placed ahead of individual rights.

Had he been alive today to defend the police chief, he might have submitted the idea that the officer was merely acting in the best interests of the state, the police force that employed him and the wider public he was employed to protect and serve.

Former Australian police officer John Blackler, co-author of "Ethical Issues in Policing",[59] presents a particularly challenging case following an event in the 1970s. During the height of a typical, scorching Australian summer a thief stole a car after the mother left the keys in the ignition while she paid for fuel at a garage service station.

Her three-year-old son was asleep on the back seat and suffering from a heavy summer cold. The thief drove off and the police were alerted immediately.

---

58   Rousseau made famous the concept of the General Will (*volonté générale*), although his critics and supporters gave a variety of conflicting interpretations of what he really meant. For more, read *The Confessions of Jean-Jacques Rousseau*. Penguin Classics, 1973.

59   John Blackler is a Research Fellow at the Centre for Applied Philosophy and Public Ethics (an Australian Research Council-funded Special Research Centre), a former New South Wales Police Officer and co-author of *Ethical Issues in Policing*. Burlington VT, Ashgate Publishing, 2006.

Officers were confident the driver would abandon the vehicle on spotting the child, but were concerned that if he abandoned the vehicle, the child could suffer heat stroke and suffocate from the heat.

As luck would have it, the thief was apprehended very quickly but refused to disclose the whereabouts of the car. One of the detectives told the suspect: *"It's been twenty minutes since you took the car—little tin box like that car—It will heat up like an oven under this sun. Another twenty minutes and the child's dead or brain damaged. Where did you dump the car?"*

Still in denial, even though he was told he could face a manslaughter charge, one of the officers landed a swift and unexpected body punch, which produced a roar of pain. The suspect retaliated and lapsed into a semi-conscious state under the ensuing rain of blows. Kneeling on hands and knees in his own urine, suffering from a pain he perhaps had never before experienced, he realised the beating would continue until he told the police where he had abandoned the child and the car. He talked.

In the case study, Blackler noted the following when the case went to trial:

> *"The police officers' statements in the prosecution brief made no mention of the beating; the location of the stolen vehicle and the infant inside it was portrayed as having been volunteered by the defendant. The defendant's counsel availed himself of this falsehood in his plea in mitigation. When found, the stolen child was dehydrated, too weak to cry; there were ice packs and rehydration in the casualty ward but no long-time prognosis on brain damage."*

This is a classic – and extremely rare –example of the ticking time bomb scenario as portrayed by Dershowitz and the pro-torture lobby. However, it is worth pointing out that if Dershowitz's torture warrant had been in existence, it could not have been executed in time to save the child's life because of the time factor involved in arranging an emergency court session and hearing. By breaking the law – for that is what the officers in the interview room did – they saved the child from almost certain death. Had the officers been charged and gone to court, their defence no doubt would have been that of doing whatever was necessary to protect and save the child. We can only speculate on the outcome of such a trial but it is fair to say that most jurors probably would have found the police actions of torture – inflicting pain for information – morally justifiable.

When in December 2005 US President George W Bush pushed through the US Patriot Act, referred to at the beginning of this book, he said it was designed *"to protect our people, our freedom, and our way of life,"* when in reality it reduced civil liberties and the freedom of individuals. Critics of Rousseau's own interpretation of the General Will could argue that the US Patriot Act is a classic example of what can happen when individuals give up personal responsibility in favour of the greater good.

Following on from that platform, it could be further argued that this sort of philosophy, left unchecked, could lead to an abandonment of personal responsibility, with highly questionable and/or controversial actions being justified on behalf of the interests of the state. A classic illustration of what can happen when this sort of justification and abrogation of individual responsibility occurs in the interests of the state unfolded in the so-called Reign of Terror,[60] when the French Revolution took a violently radical turn in September 1793. Known simply as The Terror, the following ten months were marked by mass executions of tens of thousands of so-called enemies of the revolution. More than 16,500 people were executed by guillotine in the name of liberty, equality and fraternity … the slogans of the Revolution.

Rousseau's ideas defended this period of violence by arguing that a stable government was needed to bring calm following the fall of the monarchy. Rousseau's beliefs were promoted and embraced enthusiastically by Maximilien de Robespierre[61] and other members of the Committee of Public Safety during the Reign of Terror.

The Committee began to manage the police force of the day, and The Terror was formally instituted as a legal policy by the Convention on 5 September 1793, in a proclamation which read:

"It is time that equality bore its scythe above all heads. It is time to horrify all the conspirators. So legislators, place Terror on the order of the day! Let us be in revolution, because everywhere counter-revolution is being woven by our enemies. The blade of the law should hover over all the guilty."

---

60   During the Terror, the Committee of Public Safety was set up to suppress internal counter-revolutionary activities and raise additional French military forces.

61   Among the most influential figures of the French Revolution and a key figure in the Reign of Terror. For more, see: McPhee, Peter: *Robespierre – A Revolutionary Life*. Yale University Press, 2012.

Yet despite The Terror, the French Revolution still occupies a commanding place in history as the foundation stone of modern nationalism and democracy.

More than 150 years later, an international panel of judges at the Nuremberg trials[62] threw out of court the concept of the General Will in favour of individual responsibility. Nuremberg ruled that those suspected of war crimes:

> *"Leaders, organisers, instigators and accomplices participating in the formulation or execution of a common plan or conspiracy to commit war crimes are responsible for all acts performed by any person in execution of such a plan."*[63]

It is quite clear that German minister Otto Schily was determined not to stray far from the Nuremberg principles when he publicly defended, 60 years later, the Frankfurt court's judgement. The decision to penalise the police officer who had threatened to use torture was based on these rulings of personal responsibility.

Those who criticised the senior police officer included Amnesty International and members of the Greens, the leftist partner in the German national coalition government. Wolfgang Daschner, the Frankfurt deputy police chief who was found guilty of aggravated coercion in court, received a caution and suspended sentence, thus escaping a criminal conviction, but his career was finished. Another unnamed senior officer who Daschner ordered to use "direct force" on the suspect was fined €3,600 (£2,473) and subject to a year's probation.

It is no coincidence that during her summing up on December 20 2004, Judge Baerbel Stock spoke about the history of the German constitution.[64] She said she had handed down the lightest possible sentence on the officers involved in inflicting pain on the kidnap suspect, adding that while she had no doubt of the *"honourable motive of saving a life … it must also be made clear that the laws have to be followed, including when one is in difficult situations."*

---

62 A series of military tribunals held in Nuremberg, Bavaria notable for the prosecution of prominent members of the political, military and economic leadership of the defeated Nazi Germany.

63 Nuremberg Charter, II Jurisdiction and General Principles, Article 6 (c).

64 The judge was referencing Article 1, paragraph I, which reads: "Human dignity is inviolable. All state powers must respect and protect this." This article was developed to consciously demarcate post-war Germany from the previous Nazi regime.

Meanwhile, Michael L Gross[65] approaches the ticking bomb from a slightly different, but exhaustively analytical perspective in his book Moral Dilemmas of Modern War that examines how asymmetric conflict is changing the way governments and people think about conflict. He writes of an almost symbiotic relationship between a torturer and his victim in this passage of his book:

> *"It is no surprise that human rights organizations despair of ever refuting ticking bomb or less-urgent scenarios of terrorism. Terrorism trades on abject fear, not statistics. Terrorists, therefore, have a keen interest in exaggerating the imminent threat they pose. They cannot stand before interrogators and then try to downplay the severity of the menace they present. Everyone plays into the other's hands. Terror suspects need torture to legitimate their claims and instill fear in their victims. Interrogators need terrorists and ticking bombs to defend harsh interrogation."*

Elaine Scarry[66] relies on the use of statistics to deconstruct Dershowitz's arguments in her contribution to a chapter in the book "Torture",[67] in which she names her Harvard colleague in the title in another display of the critical wrath that has descended on Dershowitz from some members of the academic community. Her argument includes this thought-provoking passage against the use of torture:

> *"In the two and a half years since September 11, 2001, five thousand foreign nationals suspected of being terrorists have been detained without access to counsel, only three of whom have ever eventually been charged with terrorism-related acts; two of these three have been acquitted. When we imagine the ticking bomb situation, does our imaginary omniscience enable us to get the information by torturing one person? Or will the numbers more closely resemble the situation of the detainees: we will be certain, and incorrect, 4,999 times that we stand in the presence of someone with the crucial data, and only get it right with the five thousandth prisoner? Will the ticking bomb still be ticking?"*

Her use of statistics is problematic, being rather self-defeating and unconvincing, since Dershowitz's theory is not limited by numbers interrogated. Quite possibly the person holding vital information could be number 5,001 or 5,021. Her main

---

65   Professor Michael L Gross is professor of political science and chair of the Department of International Relations at the University of Haifa, Israel. He is also the author of *Ethics and Activism*, 1997, *Bioethics and Armed Conflict*, 2006.

66   Elaine Scarry is the Walter M. Cabot Professor of Aesthetics and the General Theory of Value at Harvard. Author of *The Body in Pain*. Oxford University Press, 1985.

67   Levinson, Sanford: *Torture, A Collection*. Oxford University Press, 2006. Ch. 15, "Five Errors in the Reasoning of Alan Dershowitz," p. 284.

gripe appears to be that all 5,000 were held in a legal black hole without trial or charge, which is not the issue in the context of the ticking bomb. The issue is does torture work and would it work on a person holding information, which could prevent the deaths of innocents – and then justify the use of torture?

Ex-GTMO detainee Shaker Aamer has said of the numbers of the approximately 800 detainees interrogated, the one constant question was: "Where is OBL [Osama bin Laden]?" While varying methods to extract information were used, we now know the HVDs were waterboarded and worse, but none of their information led to Osama bin Laden. When bin Laden was finally located it was due to good old-fashioned intelligence gathering, foot work and electronic eavesdropping. Senator John McCain cited this effort as proof that torture simply does not work.

I have spoken to many GTMO detainees and it is clear that they felt they were tortured for information they could not give, and information they did not have; in the end, they were prepared to say anything to make the pain stop.

Although Dershowitz is probably viewed as the most prominent proponent of legalising the use of torture in the ticking bomb scenario, he is by no means a lone voice. Support comes from other academics and authors, including Australians Mirko Bagaric and Julie Clarke, who co-wrote "Torture: When the Unthinkable Is Morally Permissible".[68]

Acknowledging the Dershowitz contribution that torture should be made legal, they take things a step further, setting out their case in the introduction of their book by writing:[69]

"We argue that torture is indeed morally defensible, not just pragmatically desirable. The harm minimization rationale is used to supplement our argument. The pejorative connotation associated with torture should be abolished. A dispassionate analysis of the propriety of torture indicates that it is morally justifiable in limited circumstances. At the outset of this discussion, it is useful to encourage readers to seriously contemplate moving from the question of whether torture is ever defensible to the issue of the circumstances in which it is morally permissible."

---

68   Bagaric and Clarke: *Torture: When the Unthinkable Is Morally Permissible.*
69   Bagaric and Clarke : *Torture.*

The ticking bomb is eagerly cited by those on both sides of the argument. Jean Bethke Elshtain[70] reflects on this fact in Chapter 4 of "Torture",[71] which pulls together a compendium of thoughts from lawyers and academics on the subject. She writes:

> *"Torture remains a horror, and, in general, a tactic that is forbidden. But there are moments when this rule may be overridden. The refusal to legalize and sanction something as extreme as torture is vitally important. It follows that Alan Dershowitz's suggestion that there may be instances of 'legitimate torture' and those about to undertake it should be obliged to gain a 'torture warrant' to sanction the activity is a stunningly bad idea ... We cannot – and should not – insulate political and military leaders from often harsh demands of necessity by up-ending the moral universe: that which is rightly taboo now becomes just another piece in the armamentarium of the state."*

Elshtain is adamant that torture should remain illegal but she does not entirely distance herself from the pro-torture lobby, adding this caveat:[72] *"But 'moderate physical pressure' to save innocent lives, 'coercion' by contrast to 'torture,' is not only demanded in extreme circumstances, it is arguably the 'least bad' thing to do."*

In other words, she wants those who torture to take the full responsibility for their actions and decisions, citing as an example the case of the anti-Nazi theologian Dietrich Bonhoeffer[73] who joined a conspiracy to assassinate Adolf Hitler. Almost all involved in the plot were either shot or hanged.[74] His supporters were frustrated, she says, because he left no explanation or justification for their plans. She writes in his defence:[75]

> *"He acknowledges guilt and complicity in the name of being a Christian ... 'Civil courage,' he wrote, 'can grow only out of the free responsibility of free men.' ... The key question, for Bonhoeffer, is not 'What is the right thing for me to do?' but rather*

---

70   She is the Laura Spelman Rockefeller Professor of Social and Political Ethics in the Divinity School and also is in the Department of Political Science and the Committee on International Relations.

71   Levinson, Sanford (editor): *Torture: A Collection.* Oxford University press, 2004. Elshtain contribution: Ch. 4, "Reflection on the Problem of 'Dirty Hands,'" p. 77–89.

72   Levinson: *Torture: A Collection*, Ch. 4, p. 86.

73   A German Lutheran pastor, theologian, and anti-fascist.

74   Arrested in April 1943 by the Gestapo, Bonhoeffer was executed by hanging in April 1945, 23 days before the Nazis' surrender.

75   Levinson: *Torture: A Collection*, Ch. 4.

'What is to come?' In his circumstance, that meant what would the future hold, unless action was taken to stop it?"

Elshtain's pro-torture reasoning is dismissed by Dershowitz in a later chapter[76] of the same book, in which he attacks hypocrisies and double standards, using the example of a French officer:

"Perhaps the most extreme example of this hypocritical approach to torture comes – not surprisingly – from the French experience in Algeria. The French army used torture extensively in seeking to prevent terrorism during France's brutal war between 1955 and 1957. An officer who supervised this torture, General Paul Aussaresses, wrote an account of what he had done and seen, including the torture of dozens of Algerians. 'The best way to make a terrorist talk when he refused to say what he knew was to torture him,' he boasted. Although the book was published decades after the war was over, the general was prosecuted – but not for what he had done to the Algerians. Instead he was prosecuted for revealing what he had done and seeking to justify it."

This statement brings us almost full circle to the opening of this chapter, which began with a review of Jean Lartéguy's best-selling novel "Les Centurions" that gave prominence to the concept of the ticking bomb. One of the characters in the plot is a captain, Julien Boisfeuras, who implements torture to end the bombing campaign during the Battle of Algiers.[77] It has been claimed that he was loosely based on Paul Aussaresses, a Service de Documentation Extérieure et de Contre-Espionnage (SDECE) captain at the time. It is a claim given some oxygen by Aussaresses himself when, during an interview[78] with a journalist from the French newspaper La Monde, he admitted carrying out torture. During the interview, he said:

"Concerning the use of torture, it was tolerated, if not recommended. François Mitterrand, the Minister for Justice, had, indeed, an emissary with [French general] Massu in Judge Jean Bérard, who covered for us and who had complete knowledge of what went on in the night."

---

76   Levinson: *Torture*, Dershowitz contribution: Ch. 14, "Tortured Reasoning."

77   A campaign of guerrilla warfare carried out by the National Liberation Front (FLN) against the French Algerian authorities 1956–1957. The violence escalated when the French government deployed French forces. The use of torture resulted in a backlash against the French presence in Algeria, triggered a national debate in France and stimulated international support for the FLN.

78   "L'accablante Confession du Général Aussaresses sur la Torture en Algérie." *Le Monde*, May 3 2001. *Le Monde* online archives, accessed at http://www.lemonde.fr/cgi-bin/ACHATS/acheter.cgi?offre=ARCHIVES&type_item=ART_ARCH_30J&objet_id=702899#.

He again justified the use of torture as a small but necessary evil that had to be used to defeat a much larger evil of terrorism. Aussaresses also authored a book, "The Battle of the Casbah", in which he claimed he used these methods because it was a quick way to obtain information and defended its use by saying that the legal system was meant to deal with a peacetime France, not the counter-insurgency war with which the French army was faced in Algeria.[79] In his book, Aussaresses further contends that the French government insisted that the military in Algeria "liquidate the FLN as fast as possible." He even outlines the measures taken, including summary executions of thousands of people, hours of torture of prisoners and violent strike-breaking.

The Aussaresses book makes for very grim reading and although it could be argued that it undoubtedly romanticises and glorifies his role in the slaughter of thousands of men and women, he fails to address the metaphorical elephant in the living room ... the French lost the war in Algeria – not least of all because France could not demonstrate a moral justification for waging a war against a people who want independence for themselves. This proves the point of most military academies that tactical success is nothing without a strategic victory.

Another interesting point is that there are no passages in the book outlining any specific cases of valuable intelligence extracted under torture which would have supported Dershowitz's ticking bomb theory. It is a point Aussaresses would surely have mentioned, since the content of the book appears to hold nothing back regarding of the practice of torture.

In addition, he dismisses the democratic concept of arrest, charges and trials of those taken into French custody because that process, he said, would simply have brought the French-administered courts in Algeria to a grinding halt because of the huge numbers involved.[80]

> *"The justice system would have been paralyzed had it not been for our initiative .... Even if the law had been enforced in all its harshness, few persons would have been executed. The judicial system was not suited for such drastic conditions ... Summary execution was therefore an inseparable part of the tasks associated with keeping law and order."*

---

79   Aussaresses, Paul: *The Battle of the Casbah: Terrorism and Counter-Terrorism in Algeria, 1955–1957.* New York, Enigma Books, 2010.

80   Aussaresses: *Battle of the Casbah*, p. 127.

Quite why the US military would fete Aussaresses, Galula and Trinquier for their roles in such a spectacular failure as the war in Algeria needs to be addressed. It was certainly not lost on Petraeus when he was compiling the latest COIN manual,[81] which states quite emphatically in the "Leadership and Ethics for Counterinsurgency" section:

> *"This official condoning of torture on the part of French Army leadership had several negative consequences. It empowered the moral legitimacy of the opposition, undermined the French moral legitimacy, and caused internal fragmentation among serving officers that led to an unsuccessful coup attempt in 1962. In the end, failure to comply with moral and legal restrictions against torture severely undermined French efforts and contributed to their loss despite several significant military victories. Illegal and immoral activities made the counterinsurgents extremely vulnerable to enemy propaganda inside Algeria among the Muslim population, as well as in the United Nations and the French media. These actions also degraded the ethical climate throughout the French Army. France eventually recognized Algerian independence in July 1963."*

This passage was quoted earlier in this book but is worth repeating because of the significance of its content. While Petraeus, as the CIA chief looked for legislation to protect those under his command who might, in the future, be required to carry out EITs, here he also leaves readers in no doubt that the US military should not be engaging in such methods.

It is a view shared by American hero and 27-year veteran Lieutenant Colonel Jason Amerine, recipient of both a Bronze Star and a Purple Heart. As a captain he led his own Special Forces team in Southern Afghanistan in advance of the 2001 war, protecting Hamid Karzai as he tried to garner support for his efforts against the Taliban. An account of the top secret mission is revealed in a best-selling book by Eric Blehm.[82]

Amerine told me: *"Everything I ever learned about interrogation was completely humane, as strange as it might sound for a retired 'Green Beret' to tell you. We did one interrogation in Tarin Kowt and it entailed a gentle conversation, sharing food, and simply having a conversation. We received what information he had, then he was sent home, per Karzai's wishes for surrendering low-level Taliban."*

---

81   *The US Army Marine Corps Counterinsurgency Field Manual.* University of Chicago Press, 2007.

82   Eric Blehm: *The Only Thing Worth Dying For.* New York, HarperCollins Publishers, 2010.

It is quite clear that Amerine's approach was at odds with Aussaresses' methodology. The importance of whether Aussaresses, who retired from the French Army in 1975 with the rank of brigadier general, resembled a character in Les Centurions pales into insignificance. However, an important aspect is the way in which he carried out his "Casbah" mission and how it was received by the wider public. As news began to emerge of torture carried out by French troops under an unapologetic Aussaresses' command, the reaction by the French people sparked a national debate and brought about an end to the war, with France giving up its Algerian possession.

It is interesting to note that he, like the French revolutionary Robespierre, adopted the view that he did what he did for the sake of his country, as if to absolve himself of any personal blame. In the updated 2005 version of "Casbah", he wrote in the introduction:[83]

> *"What I did in Algeria was undertaken for my country in good faith, even though I didn't enjoy it. One must never regret anything accomplished in the line of a duty one believes in."*

He undoubtedly considered Algeria to be part of France, yet the more than a million French citizens living there became the target of Algerians fighting for what they saw as the liberation of their country.

The sordid side of Aussaresses' methods, written in stark, unrelenting detail in his book, not only earned him public rebuke in 2001 when it was published but also resulted in his being stripped of his Legion of Honor and losing the customary right of wearing his uniform.[84] Attempts to have him tried for war crimes failed. A completely unrepentant Aussaresses appeared to take full advantage of the 9/11 time line in an article[85] in The Economist. One has to wonder if such bold statements as this one would have been accepted prior to 9/11:[86]

---

83   Aussaresses, Paul: Battle of the Casbah.

84   James, Barry: "General's Confessions of Torture Stun France." *New York Times*, International Pages, May 5 2001. Accessed at http://www.nytimes.com/2001/05/05/news/05iht-france_ed3_.html.

85   "An Awkward Case: Why a Retired General's Admission about Torture in Algeria Is Embarrassing." *The Economist*, December 1 2001. Print edition. Accessed at http://www.economist.com/node/886928.

86   Aussaresses: *The Battle of the Casbah.*

"If I had bin Laden in my hands, I would do it without hesitation. In any event, I am sure every army in the world today is still employing torture."

The reaction of the French government towards its treatment of Aussaresses drew stinging criticism from Dershowitz for what he described as "hypocrisy." Ironically, Dershowitz was to find an unlikely ally in the French journalist Henri Alleg,[87] who also shared his disgust regarding the treatment of Aussaresses. In an Afterword in a new edition of his book "The Question",[88] he writes that Aussaresses:

"… was punished but not for the crimes he had committed. The amnesty laws passed decades earlier protected him from any criminal liability. Rather, the fine was levied because he bragged publicly of having perpetrated these crimes."

Of course Alleg is angry for very different reasons and goes on to express his disgust in the new edition of his book. He reveals that senior members of the French military, including Aussaresses, had gone on to export their knowledge as they pursued careers outside of the military. They were able to pass on their "particular talents" to show Latin American dictators the best methods to "suppress" populations as well as assist in advice to the South African government during the apartheid[89] years. Alleg concludes:[90]

"In various countries, including the United States, numerous intelligence officers thus received training in the tasks they would be asked to perform. They were initiated into the methods of the 'French school,' with their instructors being former torturers during the Algerian War. This 'instructional model,' which we have recently seen in operation in Iraq, at the Abu Ghraib prison and elsewhere, and at Guantanamo Bay in Cuba, is still widely emulated."

---

87   A French journalist who supported Algerian independence. He was interrogated for one month; during this time, he was put under torture, which he described in graphic detail in his book *The Question.*

88   Originally published in 1958, *The Question* is often credited with opening the torture debate in France during Algeria's war of independence and was the first book since the 18th century to be banned by the French government for political reasons. Jean-Paul Sartre's preface remains a relevant commentary on the moral and political effects of torture on both the victim and perpetrator.

89   A system of enforced racial segregation by the National Party governments of South Africa between 1948 and 1994.

90   Alleg, Henri: *The Question.* New York, Bison Books, 2010.

It is interesting to note that until the 2010 edition, Aussaresses failed to get a mention in Alleg's book. His omission appears to have irritated the former general to such an extent that he makes a derogatory reference to Alleg in his own book,[91] writing:

> *"Later on Henri Alleg, the former editor of the Communist Daily Alger Republicain, fell into a trap as he entered [Maurice] Audin's apartment [Audin was a member of the French Communist Party who 'disappeared' in Algeria in 1957]. As far as I was concerned neither Audin nor Alleg was that important, even though their names were on the file ... Audin vanished on June 21 and his disappearance caused a lot of indignation and became the object of a very detailed investigation. As for Alleg, he wrote a book, La Question, describing his interrogation. I saw him when he was placed under arrest but he failed to mention that fact in his book, which otherwise spares the reader no details."*

It could be argued that the former general's source of irritation is his pride over his activities in Algeria, for not only is he clearly proud of his "work" he also certainly appears to justify his actions using Rousseau's "volonté générale" in a section of his Foreword, which reads:

> *"I don't attempt to justify my actions, but only to explain that once a country demands its army fight an enemy who is using terror to compel an indifferent population to join its ranks and provoke a repression that will in turn outrage international public opinion, it become impossible for that army to avoid using extreme measures."*

However, there can be no justification for the brutality of the French forces according to George Andreopoulos,[92] who wrote the chapter "The Age of National Liberation Movements" in the book "The Laws of War", in 1994. He observed:[93]

> *"Nothing was to generate greater outrage in French public opinion than the stream of stories associating the French military and police forces with widespread use of torture and related practices. And it was the very use of torture that in the end*

---

91   Aussaresses: *The Battle of the Casbah.*

92   Professor of Political Science at the John Jay College of Criminal Justice of the City University of New York, where he directs the Center for International Human Rights.

93   Howard, Michael, Andreopoulos, George J, Shulman, Mark R (eds.): *The Laws of War: Constraints on Warfare in the Western World.* Ch. 11, "The Age of National Liberation Movements." New Haven CT, Yale University Press, 1994.

convinced most French people that the cause of the Algerie-Francaise was not worth the enormous strain that it was placing on the social fabric.

"The use of torture confronted France with a serious challenge to its self-image as the articulator of both the Declaration of the Rights of Man and Citizen and of the mission civilisatrice. The latter was supposed to project to the colonized people some of the values codified in the former, in particular, notions relating to constitutional government and the rule of law."

In conclusion, it appears the grand legacy of the French Revolution was under threat in the eyes of the French people, and they were not prepared to sacrifice or tarnish those principles so hard won in 1789. It now remains to be seen if the American people will react with the same sort of revulsion further down the line once the popular effects of the ticking bomb, as portrayed in movies and television series, begin to fade, along with the horrific memories of 9/11.

However, as right-wing politicians compete to become the Republican Party's presidential candidate, the use of torture seems as popular as ever, according to the Guardian newspapers.[94] A number of Republican presidential candidates both have indicated they would bring back waterboarding and other forms of "enhanced interrogation" that were dropped by the Obama Administration because they were deemed to be acts of torture.

One candidate Donald Trump was reported as saying he would "absolutely bring back" waterboarding in the fight against Daesh. *"They don't use waterboarding over there,"* he said, *"they use chopping off people's heads, they use drowning people – they put people in cages and drown them in the ocean, then lift out the cage."* The real estate billionaire added that he thought waterboarding was *"peanuts compared with what they are doing to us – what they did with [US journalist and Isis hostage] James Foley when they chopped off his head."*

Another candidate, Ben Carson, was asked if he would support Trump's call to bring back the controversial EITs and he said: *"I agree that there's no such thing as political correctness when you are fighting an enemy who wants to destroy you."*

---

94   November 22 2015 online article published on the *Guardian Newspapers* website. Accessed at http://www.theguardian.com/us-news/2015/nov/22/donald-trump-ben-carson-isis-support-waterboarding.

Perhaps more alarmingly for opponents of torture, both candidates' ratings increased following those interviews, according to a Washington Post and ABC news poll. At that time, Trump had gathered 32 percent of the support among registered Republicans and Carson 22 percent. One can only conclude that large numbers of American voters are not yet ready to regard the use of torture as unacceptable.

6
Voice of the Voiceless: Victims of Torture Have Their Say

The whole issue of torture has had a polarizing effect on those who have joined in the debate, but very few can speak from the unenviable point of personal knowledge – that is, having experienced torture first hand.

It is essential to get their views because torture victims are in an ideal position to reveal if any information they released under threat of pain, or perceived torture, provided good intelligence, saved lives or helped lead to a positive outcome for those employing such methods. The victims are also perfectly placed to talk about the long-term legacy, if any, of undergoing torture or the threat of it.

In trying to establish whether torture can ever be a useful weapon in modern warfare, those who endured it are probably better qualified than most to give valuable feedback as to its effectiveness.

Thus, this chapter is devoted to those who have experienced physical and mental torture before and during the Global War on Terror or lived with the fear that they might be tortured. Each account gives a unique perspective and can arguably contribute more to the debate on torture because the opinions in them are based on a firsthand knowledge and thus difficult to challenge – since their accounts are based on real-life experiences.

It is important to let the victims speak about torture because each testimony is unique and powerful and, since most of those quoted in this chapter thus have a wider audience than their immediate families, their testimonies and accounts potentially can reach and influence the general public.

As discussed in the previous chapter, public opinion can be a very important influence on government policy. As mentioned in that chapter, France was forced to end the occupation of Algeria when the French people began to learn about the widespread use of torture carried out by their troops.

With that in mind, it is important to note that, should their motivation for speaking truthfully and without favour be doubted, none of those interviewed in this chapter of the book has ever been charged, tried or convicted of a terror-related offence at the time of writing.

The issue of torture was confronted by the late English-American journalist Christopher Hitchens[1] for the US magazine *Vanity Fair*,[2] for which he was contributing editor until his death from cancer in December 2011. He wanted to add a new dimension to the torture debate by undergoing the experience of waterboarding for himself after which he could give a firsthand account.

After submitting himself to the practice in a controlled environment in North Carolina with military people he describes in his Vanity Fair article as *"a team of extremely hardened veterans who had confronted their country's enemies in highly arduous terrain all over the world,"* he wrote at length about the experience, concluding that waterboarding is torture.

One of his first observations challenges the popular description that the practice of waterboarding is the simulation of drowning. Hitchens, who called a halt on his own waterboarding after 11 seconds, explains:

> *"You may have read by now the official lie about this treatment, which is that it 'simulates' the feeling of drowning. This is not the case. You feel that you are drowning because you are drowning – or, rather, being drowned, albeit slowly and under controlled conditions and at the mercy (or otherwise) of those who are applying the pressure."*

But perhaps more important, he concluded his article with reinforced moral authority, having experienced waterboarding firsthand, and made the following four observations: In his view waterboarding was *"a deliberate torture technique"* adding that *"If we allow it and justify it, we cannot complain if it is employed in the future by other regimes on captive U.S. citizens. It is a method of putting American prisoners in harm's way."*

---

1   Author and journalist whose career spanned more than four decades. For more, read the article "Believe Me, It's Torture." *Vanity Fair*, August, 2008.

2   US monthly magazine of pop culture, fashion, and current affairs.

But he also observed that if it procured nothing more than "junk information" it would pose a huge question mark over the reliability of evidence, especially with regard to the case of Khalid Sheikh Mohammed, frequently referred to as the 9/11 mastermind and "KSM." Hitchens concluded that choosing torture as an option *"opens a door that cannot be closed. Once you have posed the notorious 'ticking bomb' question, and once you assume that you are in the right, what will you not do?"*

In spite of the realistic conditions he endured, all parties involved knew it was simply an exercise in which no one would die or risk being prosecuted. Nevertheless, the encounter weighed heavily on the journalist, who was regarded as an enthusiastic supporter of the Bush Administration and its actions following the events of 9/11.[3]

After his experience, he went on to write, debate and speak out against the use of torture once his article was published in Vanity Fair.[4]

I, too, have confronted the issue of torture, though unlike the Hitchens experience, I was not in a controlled, friendly and safe environment. Whilst not experiencing physical, pain-induced torture, I genuinely thought it would happen when I was arrested by the ruling Taliban in Afghanistan shortly after the events of 9/11. My account of this experience was published in a book I wrote less than a month after my release.[5]

I was arrested near Jalalabad[6] in Taliban-controlled country[7] after being discovered two days into an undercover assignment for *The Sunday Express* newspaper, where I was employed as chief reporter. Real or imagined, I was convinced that they would execute me; what really preoccupied my thoughts, though, was whether they would torture me beforehand.

---

3   Anthony, Andrew: "The Big Showdown." *The Observer*, September 18 2005. *Vanity Fair*, Review Section, p. 2. This article conveys Hitchens' political position and support very clearly.

4   Henley, Jon: "Want to Know if Waterboarding Is Torture? Ask Christopher Hitchens." *The Guardian*, July 2 2008, G2 Section, p. 2.

5   Ridley, Yvonne: *In the Hands of the Taliban*. London, Robson Books, 2001.

6   A city in eastern Afghanistan, which is the capital of Nangarhar province.

7   Before its ousting by US-led forces in 2001, the Taliban controlled some 90 percent of Afghanistan's territory, although it was never officially recognized by the United Nations.

"I decided on two things. The first being I would readily sign any confession, admitting to anything they wanted me to admit to just as long as they did not hurt me. I had made the decision ahead of any interrogation that I would give them whatever they wanted in terms of information. Secondly, if they invented a scenario I would still sign it regardless of whether it was fact or fiction."[8]

The fear of pain weighed so heavily on my thoughts during the first week I was held in Jalalabad[9] that when I found an old, rusty razor blade in a bathroom to which I was given free access, I secreted it in a bar of Chinese soap the Taliban had provided earlier, thinking that:

"The interrogations in the first two days had been very mild and no physical threats were issued during these sessions. However, I fully expected things to get rough and that torture would commence within a few days. When I saw the razor blade I saw it as an opportunity to take control of the situation by having the power to end my life. As drastic as that decision was, death by slashed wrists seemed preferable to torture.

"And I was convinced I would be tortured. What really concerned me was that I had no valuable intelligence to give and so I decided I would invent something if it meant avoiding torture or if they gave me something to sign, I would sign it regardless of content."

A few days later, one of the soldiers guarding me left his semi-automatic machine gun propped in the corner of the room and walked out. I stared at the Kalashnikov, wondering if I should pick it up and try and escape. I looked at the weapon for a long time wondering if the magazine was fully loaded, if this was a trap or just genuine carelessness on behalf of the soldier. If it was indeed a trap, had he deliberately put it there to see how I would react, if I could handle a gun? My mind was racing. In the end I decided I would probably do more damage to myself in the long run and just left it. I don't know to this day if it was a test or an error.

I later reflected that had I been tortured I probably would have seized the weapon and either shot myself or threatened others so they would shoot me. The thought of suffering through torture weighed heavily on my mind. As it turned out I was

---

8   Ridley's own notes, written in October 2001.
9   Second largest city in eastern Afghanistan as well as the centre of its social and business activity.

neither tortured nor abused but after the experience I was able to reflect on my own behaviour, reactions and state of mind during those 11 days in captivity.

Suddenly, some words I'd read by the late South African apartheid activist Steve Biko,[10] who died in police custody in Pretoria, began to resonate. He had said: *"The most potent weapon in the hands of the oppressor is the mind of the oppressed."*

Although this quotation formed part of Biko's Black Theology and Philosophy on Black Consciousness,[11] it could have been equally applicable to my own experience in detention. For although no one individual was acting as an oppressor, the fear experienced, real or imagined, was having "an oppressive effect" on my ability to think freely and rationally about the situation.

> *"Because I felt I was certainly going to die I wanted to accelerate my demise and so became the prisoner from Hell. I spat, swore and threw objects at my captors, refused to co-operate and went on hunger strike. I thought their patience would snap and they would just execute me on the spot.*

> *"Looking back I can see that the fear of torture had totally paralysed my ability to think rationally and my own imagination had completely oppressed my mind for fear of what the Taliban would do."*

With this experience still very raw, I was able to enjoy the irony presented in the autobiographical "The Battle of the Casbah" recollections of General Paul Aussaresses when he was warned of the dangers of volunteering for an assignment with the French special forces. Aussaresses, a young soldier at the time, confided in a senior officer that he accepted he ran the risk of being executed by firing squad in the event of his capture.

---

10   Biko was a well-known non-violent anti-apartheid activist who died in South African police custody in 1977. For more, read: Woods, Donald: *Biko*, Paddington Press, 1978; and Briley, John: *Cry Freedom*, London, Penguin, 1987.

11   Black Consciousness was a movement founded by Biko, which emerged in the late 1960s and was banned in 1977 in Apartheid South Africa.

The response from the senior officer was: *"My poor boy. When they shoot you'll be relieved, because they will have tortured you first. And you'll realize that torture is much less fun than death!"*[12]

That was exactly how I felt as a Taliban detainee ... that "death would be preferable to torture." It was this experience that prompted me to accept an invite to become a patron of the London-based NGO Cageprisoners until 2014. The advocacy group, known today as Cage, was launched in response to the opening of Guantanamo.

Moazzam Begg,[13] Outreach Director for Cage, is also one of the 16 former GTMO detainees from Britain who have been compensated by the UK Government[14] following their arrest, detention and ill-treatment at the hands of the US.

Begg, who says he was tortured and abused by US interrogators[15] during his captivity, adopted a rather pragmatic approach when asked about the issue of torture as outlined elsewhere in this book.

"Knowing that torture is illegal under international law, if a person carries it out then they should do it in the full knowledge that they will, some day in the future, have to be held to account for it. What cannot be accepted is that torture can be carried out and no one will accept responsibility.[16]

"I personally do not think torture works. I remember inventing a crazy story involving a Yemeni al-Qaeda plot to blow up an army barracks using a donkey laden with explosives. I remember using the term a 'suicide donkey.' I made it up just to stop the CIA from continuing their torture. I sat down long and hard thinking about what would make them happy and so I gave them this story.

---

12   The words of Captain Delmas, a French air force security officer, as recounted by Aussaresses in The Battle of the Casbah.

13   Begg was arrested in Pakistan in February 2002 and eventually renditioned to GTMO, where he remained until his release in January 2005.

14   According to "Guantanamo Civil Litigation Settlement," *Hansard*, November 16 2010, Column 752: Justice Minister Kenneth Clarke said an agreement had been reached regarding civil damages claims worth millions as part of a mediated settlement.

15   Begg, Moazzam: *Enemy Combatant*. London, Simon and Schuster UK Ltd., 2006, p. 162.

16   Begg, Moazzam: *Enemy Combatant*

"Now when I hear stories of plots being uncovered I often wonder if the perpetrator is some innocent individual who has made it all up in order to prevent being tortured. So in my view, torture is an unreliable method of gaining intelligence. Furthermore, the damage it does, in the long term, is very often irreparable.

"Many people left Guantanamo in a state of real anger at what had happened to them. In their mind they were mentally and physically tortured and if they didn't hate Americans before they were arrested, it's possible quite a few did when they left."

This observation by Begg is interesting because it implies that the torture programme inside Guantanamo could well have created terrorists who later were released to their countries. When asked to expand on this comment, he responded:

"Guantanamo will remain with the men who were held there for the rest of their lives. Most of them had never been to America but America had come to them, and Guantanamo became their only ever experience of the USA – as an occupier and jailer. Some of the humiliations endured by these men in GTMO to this day remain unspoken, undeclared. While some have described watching other prisoners beaten to death, enduring painful methods of short-shackling, sleep and sensory deprivation, body slaps and sporadic beatings, few have explained the nature of degradation they felt when being sexually abused or facing threats against their families. Witnessing everything they held sacred derided, like the Qur'an being torn and thrown into the toilet, in addition to the above, would be enough to send anyone over the edge. One soldier even told me:

"'Moazzam, if I were you, if I wasn't a terrorist before I came here, I would be by the time I left.'

"Despite this, only a few of former GTMO prisoners have 'returned to the battlefield' (if they were ever there to begin with) and that has almost exclusively been in countries where conflict and occupation [are] still in effect."[17]

Since after release, some former detainees did go on to display extreme anti-American and anti-Western sentiment by joining and/or rejoining the GWOT, it would not be unreasonable to ask if this phenomenon was a result of being radicalised by the GTMO experience.

---

17   Begg, Moazzam: *Enemy Combatant*

A report[18] from the Office of the Director of National Intelligence showed that 116 ex-GTMO detainees had "re-engaged" in fighting by March 2015. That accounts for 17.9 percent of all detainees; those who fall into this category include the Afghani Sabar Lal Melma,[19] Pakistani Abdullah Mehsud,[20] Afghani Abdul Rauf[21] and Sudanese Ibrahim Qosi.[22]

Of those four, Sabar Lal Melma, who was released from Guantanamo in 2007, had organised attacks in eastern Kunar province and funded insurgent operations, NATO spokesman Capt. Justin Brockhoff told a journalist from the Associated Press (AP).[23] He described Melma as a *"key affiliate of the al-Qaeda network"* who was in contact with senior al-Qaeda members in both Afghanistan and Pakistan, according to the AP news report published in *The Daily Mail*.[24]

After the fall of the Taliban, Melma, 49, was given the rank of brigadier general in the Afghan National Army and placed in charge of approximately 600 border security troops in Kunar, according to a file made public by WikiLeaks.[25] The contents of the file[26] included the sentence: *"Detainee was arrested due to his suspected involvement in ongoing rocket attacks on American troops."*

---

18   The Director of National Intelligence report of March 2015, entitled "Summary of the Reengagement of Detainees Formerly Held at Guantanamo Bay, Cuba" is available on the ODNI website. Accessed at http://www.dni.gov/index.php/newsroom/reports-and-publications/207-reports-publications-2015/1179-es-formerly-held-at-guantanamo-bay-cuba-2015.

19   He was arrested in August 2002 for carrying out rocket attacks against U.S. troops, transferred to GTMO in October that year and returned to Afghanistan in September 2007.

20   Mehsud spent 25 months in custody at the US base in Cuba before his release in March 2004.

21   February 10 2015 Washington Post report. Accessed at https://www.washingtonpost.com/world/national-security/us-drone-strike-in-afghanistan-kills-former-guantanamo-detainee/2015/02/10/19d9b27c-b169-11e4-886b-c22184f27c35_story.html.

22   Ibrahim al-Qosi has emerged as an al-Qaeda leader in Yemen. For more, see http://www.washingtontimes.com/news/2015/dec/31/ibrahim-al-qosi-released-from-guantanamo-emerges-a/?page=all.

23   AP: "Ex-GTMO Detainee and Key al-Qaeda Organizer Killed in Afghanistan." September 3 2011, aaccessed at http://www.dailymail.co.uk/news/article-2033254/Ex-GTMO-detainee-killed-Afghanistan.html.

24   AP: "Ex-GTMO Detainee and Key al-Qaeda Organizer Killed in Afghanistan."

25   A controversial website and not-for-profit media organisation which has leaked information using original source material – often classified – since 2007.

26   Department of Defense, Joint Task Force Guantanamo, marked secret//noforn//20300603. June 3 2005.

Another veteran of GTMO, Abdullah Mehsud, went on to become one of Pakistan's most wanted Islamic militant leaders. According to a BBC online obituary report,[27] he commanded militants who kidnapped two Chinese engineers in Pakistan's South Waziristan region shortly after his release. The BBC's Rahimullah Yusufzai[28] in Peshawar said Mehsud's long hair and daredevil nature made him a colourful character, adding that after his return from Guantanamo, Mehsud became a hero to anti-US fighters active in both Afghanistan and Pakistan.

In February 2015, *The Washington Post* carried a report that a former detainee had been killed in a US military drone strike. Abdul Rauf, who was released from Guantanamo in 2007 after spending five years there, was accused of being a recruiter for Daesh in Afghanistan, according to Rear Admiral John Kirby of the Pentagon press office.

Daesh, largely based in Iraq and Syria, had a marginal presence in Afghanistan, which Kirby described as *"nascent and aspirational."* Rauf, a former Taliban commander, swapped allegiance to the so-called Islamic State two weeks before the drone attack. Kirby said he had been planning attacks against US forces.

Although the US military and its NATO allies formally ended combat operations in Afghanistan on December 31 2014, more than 10,000 US troops remain in the country, primarily tasked with training Afghan security forces. Defending the use of drones, Kirby added: *"If they're going to threaten our interests, our allies, our partners in Afghanistan, they're fair game."*

Meanwhile, in December 2015 al-Qaeda in the Arabian Peninsula (AQAP) released a propaganda video[29] featuring former GTMO detainee Ibrahim al-Qosi, also known as Sheikh Khubayb al Sudani. In July 2010 Qosi had pleaded guilty to charges of conspiracy and material support for terrorism before a military commission. His plea was part of a deal which led to his release to his home country of Sudan in July 2012.

---

27   BBC Profile: "Abdullah Mehsud." July 24 2007, accessed at http://news.bbc.co.uk/1/hi/world/south_asia/3745962.stm.

28   Pakistan's best known and most respected journalist, according to this article: Fisk Robert: Rahimullah Yusufzai: "The Taliban respect me. I was the first journalist to visit them." *The Independent on Sunday*, March 23 2010, p. 10.

29   Thomas Joscelyn, a senior fellow at the Foundation for Defense of Democracies and the Senior Editor for The Long War Journal, writes about the video. Accessed at http://www.longwarjournal.org/archives/2015/12/ex-guantanamo-detainee-now-an-al-qaeda-leader-in-yemen.php.

It appears he joined AQAP two years later; in the video, Guardians of Sharia, he and other commanders discuss waging war. Qosi makes reference to al-Qaeda's policy of promoting individuals and small terror cells to form and then wage war against the West. The video appears to celebrate the actions of those who targeted the Parisian offices of Charlie Hebdo[30] on January 7 2015, saying the Kouachi[31] brothers were sponsored by AQAP.

The video marked the first time Qosi had been seen in public since leaving Guantanamo and returning to his family home in Sudan. He was originally captured in December 2001 as he fled the Battle of Tora Bora and detained as part of a group dubbed the "Dirty 30" by US intelligence officials.

Journalist Andy Worthington, and author of "The Guantanamo Files: The Stories of the 774 Detainees in America's Illegal Prison"[32] who wrote about the so-called Dirty 30, said of Qosi:

"Al-Qosi was a trained accountant, who had been the book-keeper for one of the businesses that Osama bin Laden ran in Sudan during his stay in al-Qosi's homeland between 1992 and 1996, and he then followed bin Laden to Afghanistan, but he was never anything more than a peripheral figure, sometimes working as a driver for bin Laden (like Salim Hamdan), and sometimes cooking at an al-Qaeda compound named Star of Jihad, in Jalalabad.

"As [journalist] Carol Rosenberg noted, he was also one of the first prisoners 'to formally allege torture,' including 'the use of strobe lights, sleep deprivation, sexual humiliation, [and] being wrapped in the Israeli flag,' in a petition filed in federal court in 2004, although that was not revealed publicly at the time, and he had to drop all allegations about his torture and abuse as part of his plea deal.

"With his long ordeal behind him, al-Qosi will return to his hometown, Atbara, north of Khartoum, where he will help to run his family's shop. Summing up his client, Paul Reichler said, 'He is an intelligent, pious, humble and sincere individual who

30   BBC round-up on the Charlie Hebdo attacks in France and other attacks which quickly followed. Accessed at http://www.bbc.co.uk/news/world-europe-30708237.

31   BBC profiles on Cherif and Said Kouachi. Accessed at http://www.bbc.co.uk/news/world-europe-30722038.

32   Website of author Andy Worthington can be accessed at http://www.andyworthington.co.uk/2010/09/15/who-are-the-remaining-prisoners-in-guantanamo-part-one-the-dirty-thirty/.

has endured much hardship the past 10 years. But he returns home without hatred or rancour.'"

Surely the question has to be asked whether torture carried out in GTMO and other US-controlled or supported sites created terrorists or recidivists? Were those ex-detainees who went on to fight in the GWOT after their release motivated by anger or revenge as a direct result of their harsh treatment? And why, as Begg said, were they reluctant to discuss some aspects of their treatment at the hands of the US?

It was a question I put to Mohammed Rebaii[33] at his home in Misrata during the Libyan revolution, where he was one of the rebel commanders in the Misrata Brigade[34] and a member of the former Libyan Islamic Fighting Group (LIFG).[35] He told me in graphic detail how he was tortured in the US detention facility at Bagram airbase in Afghanistan before being sent on a rendition flight to Libya, where he says he was further tortured by the Gadaffi regime.

"When I got to Bagram this American woman told me not to expect any 'human rights or even animal rights.' She said since 9/11 everything has changed and we were at war. I was hooded and strapped on to a giant wooden wheel and when it turned and you went in to the water you thought you'd never get back up to breathe again. I really thought I was going to drown.

"But it was the other things the Americans did to us that [were] humiliating and affected our honour. I can not speak of it to anyone but I can not forget how they degraded us. This particular form of torture was never carried out in Muslim countries, only by the Americans, and even today I do not want to tell you what they did to us and how they tried to destroy our honour."

Rebaii was adamant he was too embarrassed and "shy" to go into detail about his treatment at Bagram. He refused an offer to write down his personal experiences

---

33   Rebaii was interviewed at his home in Misrata on video in May 2012 for the purposes of
      this book about his capture and detention in Afghanistan at Bagram Air Base. An Arabic
      translator was used.

34   Made up of anti-Gadaffi forces and named after Libya's third largest city, scene of some of
      the bloodiest fighting during the 2011 revolution.

35   A group which played a key role in deposing Gadaffi; now known as the Libyan Islamic
      Movement. The LIFG was banned worldwide as an affiliate of al-Qaeda at the request of
      Gadaffi when he was regarded a keen ally of the West. However the LIFG has always
      vehemently denied any such links.

(rather than recount them in a recorded one-to-one interview). However, he then talked quite candidly about being electro-shocked and having electrodes attached to his genitals while in prison in Libya, but refused point blank to discuss his "humiliation" at the hands of the US. This refusal to go into detail would, of course, be treated with caution and possibly suspicion in a court of law, where facts and details are pivotal to evidence gathering.

However, his point-blank refusal to go into exact details about the humiliations he says he endured is repeated several times in statements given by other ex-detainees, even though the interviews were conducted in different countries and situations.

Moroccan-born British resident Tarek Derghoul,[36] another ex-GTMO detainee, said his interrogation began while he was undergoing surgery in Bagram to have a damaged toe amputated. He said:

> "I did feel they were getting pleasure from my pain in a sadistic way. They even interrogated me while a doctor amputated my toe. A woman in civilian clothes kept asking me questions while a nurse pumped some sort of liquid into my veins which kept me drowsy."

An unsympathetic observer might note the contradiction in Derghoul's comments here and wonder how he could have felt any pain, thereby giving his captors pleasure, if the anaesthetic kept him in a drowsy state. On the other hand, while it may not be what actually happened, it was the perception of Derghoul, who went on to describe his treatment in Guantanamo.

> "After that experience I felt I had to please my torturers by feeding them whatever they wanted to hear, even though it was not true. However, in Guantanamo while the physical torture was very bad the mental torture was for me much worse but I still can't talk about it.

> "I felt I was on a Hollywood film set and the only thing missing was for someone to say 'action' and when the interrogator walked in that was it, it was like a cue for action.

---

36   He was transported to GTMO in May 2002 and released without charge in the summer of 2004.

"Two nights before I was released they tried to get me to sign a paper that said I was al-Qaeda and that I promised not to go back to the battlefield and fight against them. They were filming this time but I did not sign it."

The reluctance to talk about certain aspects of their torture could prompt some cynical legal experts to dismiss their claims of pain and suffering because of a refusal to disclose hard evidence that made it difficult to measure and analyse some torture claims.

However Shaker Aamer, known universally as The "last Londoner in Guantanamo," who was released amid much fanfare and publicity in October 2015, says the torture devised by the US was far worse than the beatings and pain inflicted on him by the Afghan bounty hunters who held him captive until he was sold. As a captive prior to being detained by the US, he described how he and others were beaten regularly until their skin bled. The physical pain, he said, was preferable to the torture introduced by his American captors.

Even now, for the purposes of this book, Shaker Aamer could not and would not go into the details of the abuse he says he experienced. What he told me, however, was that none of the torture could have gone ahead without the presence of doctors and psychologists. He insists they ignored the Hippocratic oath and put their duty as soldiers in uniform ahead of the medical ethics to which they had committed.

Perhaps one of the most poignant and thought-provoking testimonies on the use of torture comes from ex-Guantanamo detainee Feroz Abassi,[37] who wrote:

"Torture is simply the torturer and the tortured. It is a relationship between two people ... In my own experience, as we were being transported from one camp to another, we were beaten without cause. Why? Some people like to dominate others physically. When Dr Aafia Siddiqui[38] was 'forcefully stripped by six men and then repeatedly sexually abused' it was not because of any justifications, pre- or post-

---

37   Arrested in Afghanistan in December 2001, he was released from GTMO without charge in January 2005.

38   This account is intriguing since the US has always vehemently denied it ever held Dr Aafia Siddiqui in Bagram after she disappeared from her home in Karachi, Pakistan in March 2003. By July 2008, she was in US custody in Afghanistan. While the Pentagon did admit it had a female prisoner, known as 650, in Bagram, the US has always said the woman, whose identity has never been revealed, was treated well at all times.

torture, that it had to be done to make her confess so innocent lives can be saved. It was simply six men who, empowered as torturers, had a legal, moral and socially acceptable way to force themselves upon a woman's private parts...

"*As Thatcher[39] put it, 'There is no such thing as society. There are individual men and women, and there are families and Adam Smith,[40] 'It is not from the benevolence of the butcher, the brewer or the baker, that we expect our dinner, but from their regard to their own interest. We address ourselves, not to their humanity but to their self-love, and never talk to them of our own necessities but of their advantages.' The same goes for the services of a torturer.*

"*This makes torture a weapon of war, just like any weapon of war. It serves to meet the collective depraved desire of this cooperative for bodies, sex, power, fame, material possessions and worship. One justification for torture is 'the ticking time bomb' theory which posits that there is a ticking time bomb and a suspect that knows where it is; an interrogator does not and therefore needs to find out because 'the greater good' of the innocent that die is of greater utilitarian value than the pain and irreparable damage the suspect will suffer.*

"*For me, I have come to believe that my torture was simply to rob me of my innocence by force so that a crime committed by a 'state,' another cooperative, the USA, could be accounted for by passing it on to me.*

In the West, 'When a crime is committed, it is committed against the state and not the individual' but what happens if it is the state that commits a crime? Who gets punished? This punishment in essence is torture.

"*In my case I was compelled to tell the truth as I did not have the 'right' to remain silent, which I would have otherwise exercised, because we had no legal protections or access to legal representatives. When I did tell the truth there was not enough in it to fabricate into a crime that the state had committed and therefore I was also forced to make things up. The interrogators blankly refused [to believe] that I was telling*

---

39   A reference to former British Prime Minister Margaret Thatcher, who made the statement during an interview for a woman's magazine in September 23 1987. For more read: "Interview for Woman's Own," Margaret Thatcher Foundation online archives. Accessed at http://www.margaretthatcher.org/archive/default.asp. For more, read: Campbell, John: *Margaret Thatcher: The Iron Lady.* London, Jonathan Cape, 2003.

40   Adam Smith, 18th century Scottish social philosopher and pioneer of political economy. For more, read: McLean, Iain. *Adam Smith, Radical and Egalitarian: An Interpretation for the 21st Century.* Edinburgh, Edinburgh University Press, 2006.

them the truth. They did not care about the truth. All they cared about was justifying the crimes of the USA and therefore they wanted a confession no matter how false."

While his fellow detainee Moazzam Begg adopted a more pragmatic stance to the use of torture, Abassi concludes:

"I would never endorse the use of torture in any circumstance because torture does not spur the mind in clarity or tongue in fluency. The torturer cannot know whether what they are being told is true or false and therefore torture does not work to gain credible information but simply extracts confessions that pass on blame of a crime by the state to another non-state actor. This leaves our thought experiment as the scenario that there is [a] ticking time bomb, a suspect that knows nothing about it and an interrogator that planted it and has the task of making the suspect admit to having done it."

None of the ex-Guantanamo or ex-Bagram detainees said they were able to provide any useful intelligence to their captors, other than stories they had invented about terrorist plots, which again raises a big question mark concerning the EITs and other methods allegedly deployed by US interrogators.

It thus could be argued that because there was no ticking bomb scenario, such torture methods were useless; in addition, the ill will and toxic legacy created by such treatment at the hands of the US could also manifest itself in a negative way. Not only could it be argued that the US lost hearts and minds over its treatment of detainees but that this revulsion could also reach beyond the detainees and their immediate circle into the wider world.

These points also were raised and endorsed by torture victim Maher Arar,[41] a Syrian-born Canadian citizen who, while changing planes in New York's JFK airport, was detained by US intelligence for 12 days. He had been visiting his wife's family in Tunisia and was on his way home to Canada when his arrest resulted in his rendition to Syria via Jordan, where he was held for a year and tortured before being released without charge and allowed to return home to

---

41   After his arrest in September 2002 he was accused of working for al-Qaeda and sent to Jordan on a private Gulfstream jet (which went via Rome, Italy) before being taken into Syrian custody and held in a Damascus prison under the control of the Syrian security services.

Canada. He since has become a cause célèbre for human rights groups, including AI, which says of his case:[42]

"A Canadian judicial inquiry confirmed that he had been tortured in Syria and considered it likely that US authorities had relied on inaccurate information provided by Canadian authorities. The inquiry also noted that thorough investigations by Canadian authorities had not in fact found 'any information that could implicate Mr. Arar in terrorist activities.' The Canadian government subsequently recognized the role Canadian officials played in his ordeal, and gave him compensation and a formal apology.

"In contrast, the USA refused categorically to cooperate with the Canadian inquiry and, although a small number of members of Congress took the initiative individually to apologize to Maher Arar via a video link to him in Canada at a committee hearing in the US House of Representatives in 2007, the US President and full Congress have failed to apologize or offer Maher Arar any form of remedy. In fact, the Department of Justice successfully fought his attempts to pursue redress in court, based not on the merits of his claim but supposed 'significant national security concerns.'"

Arar was exonerated by a Canadian government commission in September 2006,[43] which blamed faulty US intelligence. Prime Minister Stephen Harper issued a letter of apology[44] and announced that Arar would receive $10.5 million Canadian dollars in settlement for his ordeal and an additional one million dollars for legal costs.

However, the case also caused division within America as well as outside, as evidenced in this verbal attack[45] on US Attorney General Alberto Gonzales when he testified before the Senate Judiciary Committee in January 2007. Senate Judiciary Committee chairman Patrick Leahy also referred to the more widespread damaging effects caused by the Arar case:

---

42   Stated in the AI press release regarding a renewed campaign launched on June 25 2012 that urged the US government to apologise to Arar.

43   The inquiry, led by Dennis O'Connor, Associate Chief Justice of Ontario, concluded that there was no evidence to link Arar to terrorism.

44   Prime Minister of Canada Stephen Harper's Office. Press release headed: "Prime Minister releases letter of apology to Maher Arar and his family and announces completion of mediation process," January 26 2007, Ottawa, Ontario.

45   The exchange on January 17 2007 is recorded in the edited "Transcript of Gonzales-Leahy Exchange on Arar," published by the Toronto Star, January 18 2007.

"We knew damn well, if he went to Canada, he wouldn't be tortured. He'd be held. He'd be investigated. We also knew damn well, if he went to Syria, he'd be tortured. And it's beneath the dignity of this country, a country that has always been a beacon of human rights, to send somebody to another country to be tortured.

"You know, and I know, that has happened a number of times, in the past five years, by this country. It is a black mark on us. It has brought about the condemnation of some of our closest and best allies … Canadians have been our closest allies – longest unguarded frontier in the world. They're justifiably upset. They're wondering what's happened to us. Now you know and I know, we're a country with a great, great tradition of protecting people's individual liberties and rights … Let us not create more terrorism around the world by telling the world that we cannot keep up to our basic standards and beliefs."

Arar says he is still trying to get justice and some form of acknowledgement from American, Syrian and Jordanian authorities for the part each country played in his rendition. He has very strong views, as one would expect, on the question posed by me; this is what he had to say:[46]

"From my personal experience I can confirm that under torture I was ready to say anything that would please the torturers in hope they would stop the torture. Torture has certainly the potential to radicalize people. I have not developed any radical views myself but I can't speak for those who were tortured much more severely.

"The US reputation has already been damaged severely beyond repair, especially on the international stage, and more particularly in the Middle East. On one hand, the US publicly advocates for universal human rights while on the other hand it secretly violates the most basic human right of life and liberty by rendering people to brutal regimes where they are tortured and incarcerated."

As with so many victims of torture I interviewed for my research, Arar talked about the importance of receiving recognition for his suffering and what it meant to get a full and public apology from the Canadian Prime Minister. He said:

"It meant the world to me. For me an apology is an acknowledgement of the suffering I endured. It was certainly part of the long (and still ongoing) healing process. [A]few

---

46   The interview was conducted by Twitter and email on August 3 2012 after initial contact was made some weeks earlier.

members of the US Congress apologized as well but they did so in their non-official capacity."

In response to being asked about the necessity of using torture in the case of the infamous ticking bomb scenario, as portrayed in previous chapters, Arar questioned the validity of such a situation, saying:

"The ticking bomb scenario is only possible in Hollywood movies. In real life, and contrary to the self-serving claims made by many CIA officers, there is no evidence that any of the unreliable information that was obtained under torture helped save lives in a ticking bomb-like scenario. People who advocate for 'legal torture' mention the ticking bomb scenario in order to sway public opinion in favor of torture. Torture is abhorrent and should never be resorted to as an investigation tool under any circumstances."

Although relations between America and Canada were strained over the Arar case, Guantanamo has also proved to be a difficult entity for other traditional NATO allies – including Britain[47] – to accept. Some have publicly expressed the view that Guantanamo should be closed, as shown by this House of Commons exchange between Prime Minister David Cameron and a Member of Parliament on January 11 2012 and recorded in Hansard:[48]

Mike Crockart (Edinburgh West) (LibDem): *"Today, unfortunately, is the 10th anniversary of the opening of Guantanamo Bay, a despicable institution that to this day still holds one UK national. Will the Prime Minister commit to doing all he can to see that 2012 is the last year in which that institution operates?"*

The Prime Minister: *"My Right Hon. Friend the Foreign Secretary is working very hard with the United States to try to secure the issue and bring this chapter to a close. As the Hon. Gentleman will know, we have also taken steps as a Government and as a country to try to achieve some closure to what happened in the past, through a settlement with the people who were in Guantanamo Bay and through setting up a proper inquiry to ensure that the British Government were not complicit in any way in the torture of people in Guantanamo Bay or elsewhere."*

---

47   Britain has long been regarded as the closest ally of the USA and was the only major power to support America in the war with Iraq.

48   *Hansard* is the official edited verbatim report of proceedings of both the House of Commons and the House of Lords. For more, see online version, accessed at http://www.parliament.uk/about/how/publications/hansard/.

Previous Prime Minister Tony Blair remarked[49] that while the opening of Guantanamo may have been *"justifiable"* perhaps it should have been approached in a *"different way"* from a legal standpoint. Expanding on the views he sets out in his memoirs, he writes:

"The truth is that the prisoners picked up in the war zone of Afghanistan were, in a sense, prisoners of war. In normal circumstances, the war ends, they are returned; we all live peacefully ever after. Except in this case, the war hadn't ended and wasn't a conventional war. There was no way of proving, as in a proper court of law, that they were 'guilty'…

"But the whole way it was handled was done almost in the most provocative way possible, as if we deliberately sought to alienate liberal opinion rather than try to face up to the reality of the dilemma for our security."

In January 2006 German Chancellor Angela Merkel[50] said Guantanamo Bay's detention facilities "should not exist,"[51] and United Nations Human Rights head Navi Pillay issued a statement in early 2012[52] condemning the Obama administration for failing to live up to its commitment to close down GTMO.

In an extraordinary turn of events, the Obama administration now faces criticism from a number of victims of the US kidnap, rendition and torture programme with whom it may have to sit down and negotiate in the near future over shared commercial and political interests brought about by the Arab Spring.[53]

---

49   Blair: *A Journey*, p. 513.

50   For more, read: Mills, Clifford, W: *Modern World Leaders: Angela Merkel*. London, Chelsea House, 2007.

51   Merkel Pledges to Revamp Germany 'In Small Steps,'" *Der Spiegel*, September 1 2006. Online version accessed at http://www.spiegel.de/international/spiegel-interview-merkel-guantanamo-mustn-t-exist-in-long-term-a-394180.html.

52   "Pillay deeply disturbed by US failure to close Guantanamo prison." Press release issued January 23 2012 from the Office of the High Commissioner for Human Rights.

53   This term is used for the wave of peoples' revolutions which unfolded across the Arab world beginning in the Maghreb in 2011.

It is well known the US had close relations with the now disgraced Tunisian dictator Zinedine Ben Ali[54] and Egypt's dictator Hosni Mubarak,[55] whose human rights records were often challenged by international groups such as AI.[56] Their continuing close ties with Saudi Arabia, a major customer of US arms deals, and the neighbouring kingdom of Bahrain, have left the Bush and Obama administrations open to accusations of hypocrisy. According to the Human Rights Watch World Report for 2012 on Saudi Arabia:

"The US failed to publicly criticize Saudi human rights violations or its role in putting down pro-democracy protests in neighboring Bahrain. US President Barack Obama failed to mention Saudi Arabia in a major speech on the Arab uprisings and continued to pursue a $60 billion arms sale to Saudi Arabia, the biggest ever US arms sale."[57]

The irony created by the Arab Spring was not lost on former US President Jimmy Carter, who made human rights a major issue in an opinion piece he wrote for the New York Times in which he references the revolutions unfolding across the Middle East while noting that Guantanamo still remains open.[58]

"Meanwhile, the detention facility at Guantanamo Bay, Cuba, now houses 169 prisoners. About half have been cleared for release, yet have little prospect of ever obtaining their freedom. American authorities have revealed that, in order to obtain confessions, some of the few being tried (only in military courts) have been tortured by waterboarding more than 100 times or intimidated with semi-automatic weapons, power drills or threats to sexually assault their mothers. Astoundingly, these facts cannot be used as a defense by the accused, because the government claims they occurred under the cover of 'national security.' Most of the other prisoners have no prospect of ever being charged or tried either.

---

54   Under Ben Ali, Tunisia was classified as an authoritarian regime, ranking 144th out of 167 countries studied in the Economist's 2010 index on global democracy, yet it was a partner in America's GWOT and part of the Trans-Saharan Counterterrorism Initiative (TSCTI).

55   Under Mubarak, despite raising human rights concerns on a regular basis, the US gave more military aid annually ($1.5 billion) to Egypt than any other country except Israel, according to US Census Bureau Table 1299, US Foreign Economic and Military Aid by Major Recipient Country: 2001 to 2009.

56   In a June 2011 report marking 50 years of AI, the organization welcomed improved human rights situations in both countries, commenting: "with the advent of free elections in countries such as Egypt and Tunisia, human rights issues that had been banned from public discourse under previous regimes are finally being aired."

57   World Report 2012: Saudi Arabia. HRW online reference, accessed at http://www.hrw.org/world-report-2012/world-report-2012-saudi-arabia.

58   Carter, Jimmy: "A Cruel and Unusual Record," *New York Times*, Opinion Page, June 24 2012.

"At a time when popular revolutions are sweeping the globe, the United States should be strengthening, not weakening, basic rules of law and principles of justice enumerated in the Universal Declaration of Human Rights. But instead of making the world safer, America's violation of international human rights abets our enemies and alienates our friends."

The Bush Administration was forced to make some uncomfortable alliances with dictators after the events of 9/11 when the GWOT was launched, but it is interesting to note that Zinedine Ben Ali, for instance, does not receive one name check or reference in any of the political memoirs of Bush, Cheney, Rumsfeld, Rice or Rove which have been referred to several times. Could it be that the former dictator now living in exile in Saudi Arabia has become an embarrassment to the US, where once he was a close ally? Could it also be relevant that America's tolerance towards countries which do torture is measured in commercial terms – that is, arms deals and other trade benefits?

It remains to be seen if America's continuing GWOT will damage its foreign policy interests; it is very likely that in oil-rich Libya, in particular, US administrations will have to attend trade, political and commercial meetings with some of those it has been accused of torturing or being complicit in their torture. They include the key Libyan personality Abdul Hakim Belhaj[59] and his wife, who say they were both victims of US-led rendition and torture during the Gadaffi regime and have now initiated legal proceedings. The irony has not been lost on Belhaj, who willingly helped me with my research for this book when we met in May 2012 in Tripoli.

Belhaj and his wife Fatima Bouchar say they were unlawfully detained in Bangkok and renditioned to Libya in March 2004. According to hand-delivered letters from their lawyers Leigh Day & Co,[60] former Foreign Secretary Jack Straw[61] and Sir Mark Allen,[62] former director of counter-terrorism at MI6, face a series of complaints, including the following:

---

59   He was the emir of the former LIFG and became the rebel leader of the Tripoli Military Council but resigned on May 14 2012 to found the Hizb Al-Watan (The Nation Party) political party after the Libyan revolution. He spent seven years in Abu Salim prison after being handed over by the US in an operation also involving British intelligence.

60   A niche law firm specialising in complex personal injury and human rights cases. The letter of claim quoted here is referenced: SAP 81387.4 and dated January 26 2012.

61   Labour MP for Blackburn, who served as Foreign Secretary in Tony Blair's Government from 2001 to 2006.

62   Retired spymaster who joined the British Foreign Service in 1974. He was head of the MI6 Counter-terrorism unit in 2003.

- *"unlawful detention in South East Asia in March 2004 and the torture, inhuman and degrading treatment, batteries and assaults perpetrated on them by Thai and US agents during this detention;*

- *extraordinary rendition to Libya in March 2004 and the torture, inhuman and degrading treatment, batteries and assaults perpetrated on them by US agents during this flight;*

- *subsequent unlawful detention, torture, inhuman and degrading treatment, batteries and assaults perpetrated on them by the Libyan authorities (from March 2004–March 2010 in the case of Mr Belhaj and March 2004 to July 2004 for Ms Bouchar); and*

- *personal injuries and consequential losses arising from their treatment."*

Despite the ongoing legal action, Belhaj told me that he had no reservations about taking part in official government business with either Britain or America in his capacity as a leading political figure in the "new Libya."[63] He was keen to point out that as rebel commander of the Tripoli Military Council, he took part in Operation Mermaid Dawn[64] in late August 2011, which was backed and supported by NATO. While he seemed unfazed and undaunted by the prospect of working alongside those who he also accused of *"plotting"* his rendition and torture, Belhaj did reveal demands similar to other detainees interviewed for this research. He said:

"What we seek in this life is the optimal achievement of justice. We also seek the implementation of a just law that governs people and their actions. My wife and I were abducted, tortured and humiliated at Kuala Lumpur airport and later on at Bangkok airport. We were handed to the Libyan Intelligence Department which I suffered the most because of them. All of these difficulties and harassments motivate us to stand firmly by justice and the rule of law.

---

63   Belhaj's Al Watan party failed to win any seats in the country's first elections in July 2012, although he is still a senior official in the Libyan transitional government.

64   The battle for Tripoli, which began on August 20 2011, six months after the Libyan civil war started, was given the "Mermaid" codename by the rebels because the capital's nickname is "The Mermaid."

"We want to see that everyone who was involved or contributed to the violation of human rights be held accountable. My demand of [an] apology is one of my basic rights. I want the people who committed these horrible actions towards me and my wife to have the bravery and apologise for what they did."

He said his honour was violated by Americans but, like others, did not want to go into detail, although it is now widely known that much of his humiliation stems from the treatment his wife received at the hands of three hooded Americans.

She was four months pregnant, expecting the couple's first child, when, according to an interview[65] she gave to The Guardian, she was *"forced her to lie on a stretcher"* while she was tightly bound by tape by three Americans whose faces were covered by black hoods. She was then put onboard a rendition flight on a journey lasting 17 hours. She recalled that throughout: *"My left eye was closed when the tape was applied but my right eye was open, and it stayed open throughout the journey. It was agony."*

Both she and her husband were taken from Bangkok and flown to Tripoli. According to The Guardian article, documents discovered in Tripoli after the NATO bombing later revealed that the operation was initiated by British intelligence officers rather than the masked Americans.

Sir Mark Allen, the head of MI6's counter-terrorism unit, was very keen to remind the Libyans that although US intelligence had provided the plane which delivered Belhaj to Tripoli, it was only because of input by the British that he had been apprehended. He wrote:[66]

"Most importantly, I congratulate you on the safe arrival of Abu Abd Allah Sadiq [Mr Balhadj]. This was the least we could do for you and for Libya to demonstrate the remarkable relationship we have built over the years. ... The intelligence on Abu Abd Allah[67] was

---

65   Cobain, Ian. Special report: Rendition report that raises new questions about secret trials. *The Guardian*, Main Section, p. 1, April 9 2012.

66   The letter, a copy of which was handed to this author in Tripoli, was originally sent by fax to the office of Libya's then head of intelligence Musa Kusa. Simply marked: FOR THE URGENT AND PERSONAL ATTENTION OF MUSA KUSA, DEPARTMENT OF INTERNATIONAL RELATIONS AND COLLABORATION. March 18 2004. It was signed off by Sir Mark.

67   A name also used by Belhaj.

British. I know I did not pay for the air cargo. But I feel I have the right to deal with you direct on this and am very grateful for the help you are giving us."

It is likely Sir Mark may live to regret writing that particular communication and/ or sanctioning the rendition of Belhaj. It was certainly touched upon by Eliza Manningham-Buller, the former head of MI5 from 2002–2007, who wrote about the re-establishing of intelligence relations with Libya:[68] *"There are clearly questions to be answered about the various relationships that developed afterwards and whether the UK supped with a sufficiently long spoon."*

Perhaps a more important question is this one: Could the experience have a negative effect on the treatment of future detainees in post-Gadaffi Libya? According to Belhaj,[69] there would be no case of the abused becoming the abuser; he emphasised this point:

"Diagnosing the ways several intelligence organisations cooperated with the Gadaffi regime which became notorious for its violations of human rights and ruthless negligence of basic rights; all of this has simply motivated us and encouraged us to stand up against these horrific practices.

"It is our humanity that gives us the energy to oppose these practices and all the elements standing behind it. For the sake of clarity, the opposition forces in Libya are fighting for freedom and dignity. They are fighting to see their country a place [in which] to express their freedom and dignity."

Another former LIFG leader and rebel commander, Sami al Saadi,[70] outlined his experience at the hands of US agents. He has also brought a claim against MI5, MI6, the Attorney General, the Foreign Office and the Home Office for their alleged complicity in his US rendition from Hong Kong to Tripoli.

Like Belhaj, he watched helplessly, he says, as his wife and four children, ages six to 13 years, were handcuffed and flown from Hong Kong to Libya in one of the few known examples of the rendition of an entire family. His wife and children were held in a Libyan prison for two months before being released.

---

68   Manningham-Buller, Eliza: *Securing Freedom*. London, Profile Books, 2012.
69   Interview with Yvonne Ridley in Tripoli, May 2012.
70   The deputy emir of the LIFG, known by the nom de guerre Abu Munthir, spent more than six years in Abu Salim prison, Tripoli after his rendition from Hong Kong in 2004.

After the restoration of relations between Libya and the West, Gadaffi pushed the idea, which was accepted by the US and Britain, that the LIFG was linked to al-Qaeda and was therefore very much part of the GWOT. Human rights lawyer Gareth Peirce[71] said:

"Gadaffi chose to sing the song that he believed the West would like to hear, which was that all Islamic opposition to dictatorships was linked to al-Qaeda. And it was that message that effectively brought him out from the cold. Blair himself had a thesis that there was an enemy who it was Britain's obligation to eradicate, and that enemy was worldwide Islamism in its different national forms. Britain determined its narrative, true or false."

Despite these observations, Sami al Saadi viewed without trepidation having to trade, negotiate or deal with the US and its allies on an international stage. I met him in Tripoli 2012 for the purpose of my research and he told me:[72]

"Should we in the future form part of Libya's new government we will not hold back about advising America and other countries about human rights. Having experienced torture first hand, I know it does not work and no human being should have to be degraded in this way.

"We are ready to help and advise the US to move away from this barbaric practice. Libya is entering a new phase and we are determined to make our country a beacon of human rights, not just in the Arab world but in the West, too. We have to make it clear torture has no place in modern society."

One American politician who would probably embrace fully the words of Sami al Saadi is Republican Senator John McCain,[73] who knows the pain of torture after being held as a high-profile POW in North Vietnam. During his detention, he was pressured into writing an anti-American statement which said: *"I am a black criminal and I have performed the deeds of an air pirate. I almost died and the Vietnamese people saved my life, thanks to the doctors."* Once he was repatriated, McCain said

---

71 Several of her clients are former LIFG fighters turned rebels. This interview was conducted by Yvonne Ridley in June 2012 at her offices in Camden, London.

72 Interview conducted in English, with an Arab translator present, in a hotel in Tripoli, May 2012.

73 During the Vietnam War he was shot down during a bombing raid over Hanoi in October 1967, and held and tortured by the North Vietnamese until 1973 in a prison nicknamed the "Hanoi Hilton."

he bitterly regretted the statement and famously said later: *"Every man has his breaking point. I had reached mine."*[74]

McCain's suffering at the hands of the Vietnamese should not be underestimated. When a Surface to Air Missile (SAM) downed the Navy Lt. Commander, the enemy had no idea of his celebrity status as the son of a four-star Admiral.[75] According to this report McCain had ejected while his jet was upside down and suffered two broken arms and a broken leg when he was fished out of a lake in Hanoi:[76]

"Ashore, someone had smashed a rifle butt into his left shoulder, breaking it, and another had bayoneted a deep wound into his left foot. No American reached Hoa Lo in worse physical condition than McCain. Despite his wounds he was carried on a stretcher immediately to a cell in Desert Inn. Here Pigeye and Big Ugh stood over him while the cockeyed Bug interrogated him.

"Bug wanted McCain to tell him what kind of aircraft he had been flying and to name future targets. McCain kept replying with name, rank and serial number. Each time he did this, Pig Eye or Big Ugh would seize him by the neck of his T-shirt – he had been stripped to his underwear – and smash a fist into his face."

In between interrogations, McCain, unable to move because of his injuries, was left unattended in his own vomit and waste. It was only when his captors discovered his family background that he was moved to a hospital where his bones were realigned ... without anaesthetic. In 1968 he was offered his freedom but refused on seeing it would be used as a propaganda tool, and so he was regularly beaten. The torture sessions were numerous and brutal to the point where he became suicidal and wrote his infamous "confession."

It is therefore probably unsurprising that, not forgetting his own personal experience, McCain vocally opposed the use of EITs and/or any forms of torture or abuse of detainees. His attitude and determination was received with much

---

74   McCain, John: *"How the POWs Fought Back,"* U.S. News & World Report, May 14 1973, reposted in 2008 under title *"John McCain, Prisoner of War: A First-Person Account."* Retrieved January 29 2008. Reprinted in *Reporting Vietnam, Part Two: American Journalism 1969–1975*, The Library of America, 1998, p. 434–463.

75   John S McCain Jr was the commander in chief of US naval forces in Europe.

76   Hubbell, John G: *P.O.W.* McGraw-Hill Book Company, 1976, p. 363–364.

chagrin by some of his Republican colleagues, including then Vice President Dick Cheney, who recalled in his memoirs:[77]

"Despite the invaluable intelligence we were obtaining through the program of enhanced interrogation, in 2005 there was a move on Capitol Hill, led by Senators John McCain and Lindsey Graham, to end it and require that all U.S. government interrogations be conducted under the rules of the U.S. Army Field Manual ... In an effort to reach agreement with Senator McCain and explain to him how damaging his proposed amendment would be, CIA Director Porter Goss and I met with him in a secure conference room at the Capitol and tried to brief him about the program and the critical intelligence we had gained. But John didn't want to hear what we had to say.

"We had hardly started when he lost his temper and stormed out of the meeting. His opinion carried a good deal of weight because he had been a prisoner of war ..."

In May 2011 the debate over torture was reignited again in America over the death of the al-Qaeda leader Osama bin Laden. Former US Attorney General Michael B Mukasey had said that EITs had led to bin Laden's bloody demise in a house in Abbottabad in Pakistan where he had been hiding[78]– a claim which saw McCain quickly re-enter the debate and say:[79]

"Much of this debate is a definitional one: whether any or all of these methods constitute torture. I believe some of them do, especially waterboarding, which is a mock execution and thus an exquisite form of torture. As such, they are prohibited by American laws and values, and I oppose them ...

"But this must be an informed debate. Former Attorney General Michael Mukasey recently claimed 'the intelligence that led to bin Ladin ... began with a disclosure from Khalid Sheik Mohammed, who broke like a dam under the pressure of harsh interrogation techniques that included waterboarding. He loosed a torrent of information – including eventually the nickname of a trusted courier of bin Ladin.' That is false."

---

77   Cheney: *In My Time*, p. 359–360.

78   Mukasey, Michael B: "The Waterboarding Trail to bin Ladin." *The Wall Street Journal*, Opinion page, May 6 2011.

79   McCain, John: "Bin Ladin's Death and the Debate over Torture." *Washington Post*, Opinion page, May 12 2011.

McCain says he based this statement on a conversation he had with the CIA's Director Leon Panetta; again, drawing on his own personal experiences as a victim of torture, he eagerly says that such abuse produces poor intelligence: *"… under torture a person will say anything he thinks his captors want to hear – true or false – if he believes it will relieve his suffering."*

While other victims of torture have used the argument that it could radicalise or even create terrorists, the US Senator expressed additional fears in the same article, which had not yet been raised by others:

> *"Mistreatment of enemy prisoners endangers our own troops, who might someday be held captive. While some enemies, and al-Qaeda surely, will never be bound by the principle of reciprocity, we should have concern for those Americans captured by more conventional enemies, if not in this war then in the next."*

McCain was tortured into confessing and writing anti-American propaganda for his North Vietnamese captors during the Vietnam War because, as he said, he had reached his *"breaking point."*

What his captors did not realise was that after taking him to the brink of death physically and mentally, and getting him to sign their anti-American message, McCain had crossed another Rubicon. Hubbell takes up the story:[80]

> *"His captors, doubtless in the certainty that they could rely on him for additional contributions in the future, allowed him to rest. This was a mistake. For two weeks he gathered his strength and mobilized his spiritual resources. Then they came back to him for another statement, and he was able to refuse. They were never able to break McCain again."*

If the graphic accounts outlined so far are to be believed, then torture produces nothing more than false confessions and unreliable intelligence. Individuals as diverse as Vietnam War veteran Senator John McCain, ex-GTMO detainee Moazzam Begg, Libyan dissident Abdulhakim Belhaj and the late Christopher Hitchens all believed torture was an unreliable method of obtaining information.

---

80   Hubbell: *P.O.W.*, p. 454.

The following pages will focus in more detail on two other torture victims: KSM and Ibn Sheikh al-Libi, the first senior al-Qaeda suspect picked up in Afghanistan in November 2001 after the GWOT had begun.

Unlike the previous case studies, the innocence or guilt of these two can not be determined, as one – KSM – has yet to be tried and the other is dead. However, both of these cases are pivotal to the argument that torture not only produces flawed information and false confessions but can set in motion serious repercussions which could create a toxic legacy in the wider world, far beyond the immediate discomfort factor experienced by victims of torture.

It is a view shared in part by the late Lieutenant-Colonel Robin William George Stephens,[81] one-time head of a top secret British detention facility during World War II and the author of the now declassified document "A Digest of Ham."[82] His meticulous records, which are now available at Britain's National Archives in Kew, West London, are also available in book form. The contents show, in great detail, exactly how MI5 conducted its interrogations and its methods of interrogation, including its successes and failures during the Second World War.

The once top secret files on Camp 020 reveal the story of Latchmere House, MI5's holding centre for captured enemy agents. Stephens' records show that more than 400 suspected spies passed through his hands. Most, according to him, were "broken"; some became double-agents and a few were executed for treason.

Like Guantanamo, this camp was held outside of the Geneva Convention and not listed by the Red Cross. As far as British intelligence was concerned, it did not officially exist until the Public Records Office at Kew opened its archives in 1999.

"A Digest of Ham," containing Stephens' own personal observations, also reveals his methods of extracting information using psychological techniques and games,

---

81   Known affectionately as "Tin Eye" Stephens, he was an extrovert Commandant of Camp 020 from 1940–45, a secret detention facility run by MI5 where wartime interrogations were conducted.

82   The manuscript, written in 1946, was MI5's secret official history on the spy prison near Ham Common in Richmond, London until it was handed over to the Public Records Office (PRO) on September 16 1999. A year later it was published in book form: Stephens, RWG: *Camp 020, MI5 and the Nazi Spies.* Kew, Public Records Office, 2000.

including the stool pigeon,[83] cross-ruff[84] and sympathy men.[85] However, for the purposes of this research the interesting thing to note is that physical violence was never used, according to the Colonel, apart from a rogue interrogator. Writing about interrogation techniques, he said:

"What should be the attitude of the interrogator? The bitter, uncompromising approach is as effective as any. And as with a man, so with a woman – no quarter. And often how profitable, the instant there is a glimmering of an admission, to make the man write it down. Still standing, he can write down the second admission, and the third, until the cumulative effect undermines his morale. How easy to wriggle out of a verbal lapse; how difficult to erase a written admission? Such admissions, one after another, are the milestone[s] on the road to surrender. Pressure must be maintained.

"Pressure is attained by personality, tone and rapidity of question; insistence upon an immediate answer, recapitulation. The requirement is a driving attack in the nature of blast which will scare a man out of his wits.

"Again, as with a man, so with a woman. There is no room for chivalry in modern espionage. Never promise, never bargain. The man's neck is in your grasp. Never forget it; never let him forget it.

"Never strike a man. For one thing it is the act of a coward. For another, it is unintelligent, for the spy will give an answer to please, an answer to escape punishment. And having given a false answer, all else depends upon a false premise."[86]

In another passage the colonel wrote:

---

83   Refers to the use of a decoy or informer who tries to gain the trust of a detainee; the hunting practice of fixing a dead or replica pigeon on to a stool to act as a decoy to attract other birds.

84   A ploy used in the case of joint spies, where both are separated while each is convinced the other has talked.

85   With this technique, the interrogator would try and gain the confidence of a POW by expressing sympathy over his plight, sometimes in the guise of a welfare officer and a position of trust.

86   Stephens: *Camp* 020, p. 118.

"For interrogation there is not a golden road to success ... Patience and perseverance are not without value, as success in one case was achieved after seventy-seven days. Violence is taboo, for not only does it produce an answer to please, but it lowers the standard of information."

Of the rogue interrogator who crossed a line, while his identity still remains classified, it is clear his violent response to a detainee was not acceptable. In Volume Two of Case Histories by Colonel Stephens, his account about a German spy called Tate is as follows:

"Tate made no admission under police interrogation. He arrived at Camp 020 on 21 of September. The case had aroused such interest that three outside case officers were permitted, at the request of MI5, to undertake the initial interrogation. It proved abortive. The external intervention of the interrogation had not been happy. Now one of the visitors followed Tate to his cell at the close of that first interrogation and, in flagrant violation of the Commandant's rigid rules that no physical violence should ever be used at Ham, struck the agent on the head. The incident led, on immediate representations by the Commandant, to the instant recall of the visitors from the camp."

These views of non-violent interrogation were endorsed more than six decades later by Eliza Manningham-Buller, who was equally adamant about the use of torture, saying it should be totally rejected "even when it may offer the prospect of saving lives." The former head of MI5, who would almost certainly have read Stephens' manuscript before it was declassified, added:[87]

"I am proud my Service refused to turn to the torture of high-level German prisoners in the Second World War, when, in the early years, we stood alone and there was a high risk of our being invaded and becoming a Nazi province. So if not then, why should it be justified now?"

It is clear from the contents of Stephens' manuscript that he enforced an ethos of non-violence at Camp 020. Ironically, as word spread of its success there were visits from US intelligence agencies and the US military to see the British methodology. However, critics of all forms of torture could put forward the argument that psychological stress is also a form of torture. Interestingly, Stephens'

---

87   Manningham-Buller: *Securing Freedom*, p. 49.

book is listed on the American spy agency's *"The Intelligence Officers Bookshelf"*[88] as recommended by Hayden Peake, the curator of the CIA's Historical Intelligence Collection.

High-profile US visits included those from Major-General Clayton L. Bissel and Brigadier-General Franklin C. Sibert. Stephens added:

> *"The upshot of these visits was that Ham would cover the American requirements until they themselves could set up a similar organization in France. In the meantime US Army officers were detailed to Ham to gain whatever insight into the work time would permit. Good comrades and very intelligent they were, and it is hoped they liked us one half as much as we liked them."*

It is not known if Stephens' methods were studied and read by the CIA in particular but, if they were, then his methodology and practices appear to have been ignored by the team of agents involved in EITs and specifically the interrogation of the suspected mastermind of 9/11 and key al-Qaeda operative known as KSM. Captured in the military garrison town of Rawalpindi, Pakistan on March 1 2003, declassified US documents now reveal he was tortured, including being waterboarded 183 times.[89]

On page 37 of the Office of Legal Counsel (OCL) memo, in a passage discussing the differences between the Survival, Evasion, Resistance and Escape programme (SERE techniques) and the torture used with detainees, the memo explains: *"The CIA used the waterboard 'at least 83 times during August 2002' in the interrogation of Zubaydah. IG Report at [page] 90, and 183 times during March 2003 in the interrogation of KSM."*

Page 15 of the same memo, written by Steven Bradbury, head of the OLC, to John Rizzo, the Senior Deputy General Counsel of the CIA, makes clear the US policy regarding the use of the waterboard. The rules limit waterboarding to no more than 60 times per month, yet this was clearly not the case for KSM's programme.

---

88   This archive, not classified, is held in the CIA's Center for the Study of Intelligence (CSI) at the agency headquarters in Langley, Virginia.

89   A 2005 U.S. Justice Department memo released in April 2009 stated that Mohammed had undergone waterboarding 183 times in March 2003. Ref: *Application of United States Obligations Under Article 16 of the Convention Against Torture to Certain Techniques that May Be Used in the Interrogation of High-Value al-Qaeda Detainees.* US DoJ, OLC May 30 2005. 0000011.

We now know from archival material that US President Obama suspended the use of waterboarding on his second day in office, declaring it to be torture. The Bradbury memo makes it clear that even the EIT rules laid down by the OLC appear to have been broken.

Thus, it is difficult to judge the success of the KSM confessions, which were prolific, according to former US President George W Bush's memoirs, in which he writes:[90]

"Khalid Sheikh Mohammed proved difficult to break. But when he did, he gave us a lot. He disclosed plans to attack American targets with anthrax and directed us to three people involved in the al-Qaeda biological weapons program. He provided information that led to the capture of Hambali, the chief of al-Qaeda's most dangerous affiliate in Southeast Asia and the architect of the Bali terrorist attack that killed 202 people.

"He provided further details that led agents to Hambali's brother, who had been grooming operatives to carry out another attack inside the United States, possibly a West Coast version of 9/11 in which terrorists flew a hijacked plane into the Library Tower at Los Angeles ... The intelligence he provided, which proved vital to saving American lives, almost certainly would not have come to light without the CIA's enhanced interrogation program."

This impressive list of crimes normally should be accounted for in a court of law; however, according to some legal experts, the use of torture and excessive use of waterboarding on KSM makes it impossible to pursue a successful prosecution through the courts. British lawyer Roger Smith[91] explains why:

"I believe that Khalid Sheikh Mohammed (KSM) is guilty of conspiracy to murder 2,977 people in, and over, the US on 11 September 2001. What is much more outrageous is that the US, by its treatment of him, has foresworn any chance of legitimacy for the process of his prosecution and punishment.

"You cannot opt in and out of human rights. KSM was subject to simulated drowning 183 times ... Actually, KSM gave more information to FBI agents using conventional interview techniques than he ever did to the CIA. His treatment has raised all sorts

---

90   Bush: *Decision Points*, p. 170–171.
91   Director of Justice, the all-party law reform organisation dedicated to advancing access to justice, human rights and the rule of law.

of doubts over his admissions – among them the personal slitting of the throat of US journalist, Daniel Pearl. Is he covering for others? Did he admit to stop the pain? These doubts disturb not only lily-livered liberals but hard-bitten FBI interrogators who regard the CIA squad as goons out of control."[92]

Would KSM have cracked under Col. Stephens' more subtle approach to interrogation in Camp 020? It is impossible to say, but if that approach had been adopted, the successful prosecution of KSM in a conventional court of law would be a much more plausible prospect today. As it stands now, it appears as a result of the EITs conducted on KSM, most of the information gathered is viewed as completely useless in legal proceedings. That is certainly the view of US investigative journalists Terry McDermott and Josh Meyer, whose book[93] charts the decade-long US effort to track down the man described as the chief operating officer of al-Qaeda.[94]

During a Q & A put to them in the promotional literature for their book tour in the US, the two responded with these words to a question asking how they felt the KSM investigation was mishandled after his capture:

"The CIA's decision to incorporate torture into its interrogation program made almost all the information gathered from the interrogations suspect in its truthfulness and useless in legal proceedings. KSM brags about how he was able to game the interrogation sessions and how he was able to obscure information and send investigators on wild goose chases."[95]

The case of KSM polarises people, from those who have little or no interest in the Pakistani's sufferings to those who are vehemently opposed to torture; for the purposes of this book, however, the treatment of KSM makes an ideal study when seeking an answer to the question about the effectiveness of torture.

---

92   Smith, Roger: "Taint of Torture Remains Despite Overlay of Legal Process." *Law Society Gazette*, Op-ed page, May 17 2012.

93   McDermott, Terry and Meyer, Josh: *The Hunt for KSM. New York*, Little, Brown and Company, 2012.

94   Description by Peter Bergen, author of *The Longest War: The Enduring Conflict between America and Al-Qaeda*. Free Press, 2011.

95   Given in a 10-page press release in March 2012 by publishers Little, Brown and Company: *The Hunt for KSM; Inside the Pursuit and Takedown of the Real 9/11 Mastermind, Khalid Sheikh Mohammed*.

What is not disputed is the prolific nature of his confessions, some of which were outlined within the pages of the Bush memoirs. If McDermott and Meyer are correct in questioning the validity of those confessions, however, then the observations made in the previous chapter by victims of torture increase in their relevance.

> *"KSM spoke voluminously ... The torture and interrogations produced more information than investigators could competently track down. Much, if not most, of the information was bad – made up, KSM would later say, so the torture would stop. From the outset, in fact, the written reports of his interrogations that were sent back to Langley contained a warning at the top that the detainee had a history of lies and fabrications."[96]*

Their views were indeed backed up by KSM himself, who wrote in an ICRC report[97] subsequently leaked and reprinted in The New York Review of Books two years later:[98]

> *"During the harshest period of my interrogation I gave a lot of false information in order to satisfy what I believed the interrogators wished to hear in order to make the ill-treatment stop. I later told the interrogators that their methods were stupid and counterproductive. I'm sure that the false information I was forced to invent in order to make the ill-treatment stop wasted a lot of their time and led to several false red-alerts being placed in the US."*

It is what KSM did not reveal that troubled his CIA interrogators and, judging from the title, they acknowledged as much in a classified document handed over to the 9/11 Commission: CIA report, Intelligence Community Terrorist Threat Assessment, "Khalid Shaykh Muhammed's Threat Reporting – Precious Truths, Surrounded by a Bodyguard of Lies."[99] The title of the document echoed a famous comment by World War II leader Sir Winston Churchill when he said:

---

96   McDermott and Meyer: *KSM*, p. 267–268.

97   ICRC report on the Treatment of the Fourteen "*High-Value Detainees*" in CIA Custody, February 2007.

98   Danner, Mark: *The Red Cross Torture Report: What it Means*, April 30 2009, p. 43.

99   This document was compiled on April 3 2003 but its contents are still classified and its reference was redacted in the 9/11 Commission Report on the terrorist attacks against the US.

"In wartime, truth is so precious that she should always be attended by a bodyguard of lies."[100]

However, KSM was not protecting the national interests of a country and its citizens; he was, it appears, protecting the al-Qaeda leadership and its terror network. Despite repeated questioning focusing on the whereabouts of the al-Qaeda leader Osama bin Laden, he gave his interrogators little or nothing, as previously established by US Senator John McCain:

"'He had us chasing the goddamn geese in Central Park because he said some of them had explosives stuffed up their ass,' Ali Soufan, the FBI counter-terrorism agent, said. He was exaggerating, he conceded, but not by much. KSM's claims of al-Qaeda's nuclear and WMD [weapons of mass destruction] capabilities had the CIA and the FBI especially spun up, but after frantic and intensive deployments around the world, it was determined that KSM was making up almost all of it."[101]

Soufan, who published his memoirs on the 10th anniversary of 9/11, quit the FBI in 2005, partly in anger, he says, over the introduction of EITs, which he blames for a delay in the success of the hunt for Osama bin Laden. Speaking after the death of bin Laden in May 2011, he said:[102]

"This case is the biggest proof that waterboarding and enhanced interrogation techniques did not work at all. And I saw it firsthand. It actually delayed the hunt for bin Ladin. A name of his courier came up in 2002, before Khalid Sheik Muhammad was arrested. He knew everything about the guy, and he lied about it! If waterboarding worked, KSM would have said the guy's real name back in March 2003."

Expanding on that theme, Soufan gave many more interviews, including a Q&A in *Der Spiegel* magazine in which again he was highly critical of the CIA's interrogation techniques,[103]according to this section:

---

100   Churchill said this to Stalin in 1943 at a conference in Tehran to stress the need to keep the Allies' plans for D-Day secret. For more, read: Churchill, Winston: *Memoirs of the Second World War.* Boston MA, Houghton Mifflin, 1990.

101   McDermott, and Meyer: *KSM*, p. 270.

102   Smith, Chris: "Did Waterboarding Lead to Bin Ladin's Lair? Ex-FBI Specialist Says 'No Way.'" *New York News & Features Daily Intel* blog. Accessed at http://nymag.com/daily/intel/2011/05/did_waterboarding_lead_to_bin.html.

103   Sandberg, Britta: "We Did Exactly What Al-Qaeda Wanted Us To Do." *Der Spiegel* Magazine, Cover Story, September 11 2011.

SPIEGEL: *"In your book, you also criticize the fact that the US never really understood its enemy al-Qaeda."*

Soufan: *"I think we definitely underestimated the ideological motivations for these groups: what makes people blow themselves up, the religious signification of al-Qaeda. It's not politics. The Chinese military strategist Sun Tzu said a long time ago: 'If you know your enemy and know yourself, you will win a hundred times in a hundred battles.' Unfortunately with the War on Terror we forgot who we are, but also we didn't know our enemy. Look at al-Qaeda. On the eve of 9/11, they had about 400 operatives. They led us into a war longer than World War I and World War II. Not because they are such smart people, but because we did not understand our enemy. Instead, we applied waterboarding and enhanced interrogation techniques. We did exactly what al-Qaeda wanted us to do. When you do this, what are you proving to the guy? You're proving that everything he thinks about you is right. But if you come with a cup of tea, he doesn't know how to act."*

SPIEGEL: *"That was your strategy as an interrogator, to come along with a cup of tea?"*

Soufan: *"Every interrogation is different. You have to get them out of their comfort zone. Even if conditions are harsh, it can still be a comfort zone. Because you behave like they expect the enemy to behave. You have to confuse them. I interrogated bin Ladin's driver, Salim Hamdan, in Guantanamo. Another American before me had promised him that he could make a phone call to his wife. But he never could. When we came, he said to us: 'All of you Americans, you are lying.' And we found out that indeed they did not fulfill the promise they made. I said to him, 'OK, we messed up. Sorry, I apologize.' And I gave him the phone."*

SPIEGEL: *"Did your method work?"*

Soufan: *"He couldn't believe it. But after he made the phone call and he heard his wife's voice, he kneeled and started crying and thanked God. We took him back, we gave him some water, tea. For about 20 minutes he didn't say a word. And then he started asking me about Yemen and then said: 'OK, what do you want to know?'"*

Unsurprisingly, the CIA's response to Soufan's accusations and criticisms were not received with good grace by the agency; as well as ordering redactions in the book, Preston Golson, a CIA spokesman, issued a rebuttal in a New York Times interview. He said Ali Soufan's accusations in his memoirs had diminished:[104]

> *"..the hard work and dedication of countless C.I.A. officers who have worked tirelessly against al-Qaeda both before and after 9/11 – hard work that culminated in the operation that found Bin Ladin. With all due respect to Mr. Soufan, the Central Intelligence Agency has a very different assessment, as you might expect, on these events."*

The rebuttal was not unexpected, but Soufan stood by his methods. According to the Arabic-speaking, Lebanese-born agent, he disarmed prisoners by addressing them in their native language, using their family nicknames and surprising them with details they did not expect him to know. In addition, he says he brought them their favorite foods. Perhaps more important, he also employed the same sort of subterfuge which had worked so well in Camp 020 by using the cross-ruff ruse by persuading detainees that their associates had already talked. He showed one prisoner a doctored photograph and persuaded another that a colleague was a "human polygraph" who could tell when the prisoner was lying.

However, it is also clear from journalist Ian Cobain's book[105] that war-time Britain did rely on the use of torture in other institutions, employing violent interrogation tactics, mock executions and sleep deprivation on POWs.

In an extract from a Daily Mail article, Cobain wrote:

> *"It was in 2005 during my work as an investigative reporter that I came across a veiled mention of a World War II detention centre known as the London Cage. It took a number of Freedom of Information requests to the Foreign Office before government files were reluctantly handed over.*

> *"From these, a sinister world unfolded – of a torture centre that the British military operated throughout the Forties, in complete secrecy, in the heart of one of the most exclusive neighbourhoods in the capital. Thousands of Germans passed through the unit that became known as the London Cage, where they were beaten, deprived of sleep and forced to assume stress positions for days at a time.*

104   Shane, Scott: "9/11 May Have Been Stopped but for High-Level Dysfunction, Ex-F.B.I. Agent Writes." *The New York Times*, p. A25, September 12 2011.

105   Cobain, Ian: *Cruel Britannia*, London, Portobello Books, 2012.

"Some were told they were to be murdered and their bodies quietly buried. Others were threatened with unnecessary surgery carried out by people with no medical qualifications. Guards boasted that they were 'the English Gestapo.' The London Cage was part of a network of nine 'cages' around Britain run by the Prisoner of War Interrogation Section (PWIS), which came under the jurisdiction of the Directorate of Military Intelligence."

In the meantime, only the passage of time will tell if justice will be served in the case of KSM; for the purposes of this research, the focus remains on quantifying the success or lack of it over the use of torture. If he is the mastermind of all of the atrocities and possible future terror attacks, as claimed by some sections of US intelligence, then his mere removal from the "playing field" is a victory in itself. However, the question to ask is what the waterboarding and other EITs did achieve from a positive point of view, and that may prove difficult to quantify in absolute terms.

 Another intriguing case centres on the Libyan-born Ibn Sheikh al-Libi,[106] who was captured in Pakistan and handed over to the US military in November 2001 following the collapse of the Taliban regime. He was the emir or leader of the Al Khaldan training camp in Afghanistan; thus, he was regarded as a highly prized asset when he was taken by US forces to Bagram.

Sheikh Mohammed Bosidra recalled in an interview[107] details and information as told to him by Ibn Sheikh when they were held in the same cell block in Abu Salim Prison in Libya:

"He told me how he was surprised as he entered the American base because rock music was being played very loudly and the words to the song had been changed to 'we have caught Ibn Sheikh.' He told me later he could not understand what all the fuss was about as he did not consider himself a highly prized prisoner at all.

"He had nothing to do with al-Qaeda or Osama bin Ladin since he declared his '98 fatwa[108] against the United States. After this happened the Taliban told him that all

---

106   Born in Ajdibya as Ali Mohamed al-Fakheri.

107   A religious leader in Benghazi who met Ibn Sheikh in Abu Salim Prison in Tripoli in 2008, a
       year before he died. Interview, filmed for purposes of this book in a hotel room in Benghazi
       in March 2011 during the Libyan Revolution.

108   Sent to al-Quds al-Arabi newspaper in London via fax on February 23 1998 declaring war on
       the West and Israel, signed by OBL and four other terror groups. An English translation can
       be read online at PBS. Accessed at http://www.pbs.org/newshour/terrorism/international/
       fatwa_1998.html.

the training camps would come under the control of OBL and he would have to join bin Ladin or close down his camp.

"He decided to close down his camp. It operated mainly to train fighters for the jihads in Kashmir and Chechnya. He decided to remain in Afghanistan because as an enemy of the Gadaffi regime it was not safe for him to return to Libya. He wasn't with the LIFG, nor was he with al-Qaeda but the Americans refused to accept this."

If the accounts of Bosidra and other former prisoners who also spoke with him are to be believed, al-Libi told them he was sent on a merry-go-round of ghost prisons across the Maghreb, including Morocco, as well as Diego Garcia, Alaska, a site in Europe and Guantanamo Bay. Bosidra summed it up by saying:

"In Cairo they sliced his flesh with a blade that was infected with Hepatitis C. They drilled his skin and they tried to bend his back to the point of breaking by bringing his ankles over his head.

"In Alaska, they were polite and let him watch American sports on TV, that's all there was. When he stepped off the plane there he was so cold they put six layers of socks on his bare feet.

"In Guantanamo, after they diagnosed hepatitis, the doctors offered no treatment other than honey.

"When he left Bagram for Cairo, a CIA man locked him in a casket naked but abused him and said he was going to rape his wife and mother. He told him he was going somewhere where they would make him talk. 15 hours later he was in Egypt."

Mohamed Rebaii,[109] who first saw him in detention in Bagram in 2003, and later saw him in Abu Salim Prison, said that the worst type of pain and tortures were inflicted on al-Libi in Cairo by his account.

---

109   He was moved on August 22 2004 to Libya and did not see al-Libi again until 2007, when he was sent to Abu Salim Prison. This interview was conducted at Rebaii's home in Misrata in June 2012 for this book.

"He told me they drilled his flesh and he showed me the marks on his body. He said he tried to resist the torture and could not because it went on for a month and so he told them what they wanted to hear. He said the al-Qaeda had relations with Saddam and they were working together.

"When he realised his confession was used to start the war in Iraq he didn't feel guilty or ashamed. He said everyone knew the US wanted a war in Iraq and if it had not been him, someone else would have confessed to the lies.

"All during his captivity he had dark times, but the darkest days in terms of torture were in Egypt. When he was held in Guantanamo, he told me he was given a choice to go to Israel or Cairo and he told me he chose Cairo because as a Muslim, he was convinced they would show him mercy.

"The worst of the mental torture, he says, happened in Bagram because the Americans insulted his dignity and played with his body in a demeaning way. I can not go into the detail."

The author has not yet received responses from requests made through FOIA to US authorities, despite FOIA being activated from the summer of 2011 for the purposes of this research.

However, Bosidra's account of al-Libi being taken to Guantanamo has now been corroborated by ex-GTMO detainee Shaker Aamer, who confirmed to me that the Libyan had indeed been rendered to the facility. He also corroborated that while at the Cuban base, officers from British intelligence had interviewed al-Libi.[110]

The US intelligence community remembers al-Libi's case well, usually in negative terms. When he initially entered Bagram in December 2001 he was handed over to FBI interrogators, who described him as a potential "goldmine"[111] because of his connections with the Khalden training camp.

"At the FBI's field office in New York, Jack Cloonan thought they had a possible gold mine. He knew that Zacarias Moussaoui and Richard Reid, the so-called 'Shoe

110   Interview with Yvonne Ridley at his home in London on January 20 2016.

111   Mayer, Jane: *The Dark Side: The Inside Story of How the War on Terror Turned into a War on American Ideals.* New York, Doubleday, 2008, p. 104.

Bomber,' who attempted to detonate plastic explosives while in-flight on American Airlines Flight 63 from Paris to Miami on December 20, 2001, both of whom were in U.S. custody, had spent time at Khalden camp.

"Cloonan worried that 'neither the Moussaoui case nor the Reid case was a slam dunk.' But if they could turn al-Libi into a state's witness, he thought, it could make all the difference."

The FBI were said to be very excited by the detention of al-Libi and, according to Jane Mayer's book, two of their agents, Russell Fincher and Marty Mahon, set about interviewing him – but not before reading him his rights. Cloonan recalls in *The Dark Side*:[112]

"I told them, 'Do yourself a favor, read the guy his rights. It may be old-fashioned, but this will come out if we don't. It may take ten years, but it will hurt you, and the Bureau's reputation, if you don't. Have it standing as a shining example of what we feel is right.'"

The "Camp 020"-style approach appeared to work on al-Libi who, according to Mayer's FBI sources, gave *"specific, actionable, intelligence – information that could save American lives"* – so much so that al-Libi asked the agents if he could be part of the witness-relocation programme, which would enable his Syrian-born wife and daughter to move to the USA, according to the same sources.

Although no deal was ever made, it appears a battle was played out in Washington over which intelligence agency should have full custody of al-Libi. As recounted in Mayer's book, the FBI lost their prized asset to the CIA, despite their protests. In his own memoirs, the former head of CIA George Tenet writes:[113]

"We believed that al-Libi was withholding critical threat information at the time, so we transferred him to a third country for a further debriefing. Allegations were made that we did so knowing he would be tortured, but this is false. The country in question understood and agreed that they would hold al-Libi for a limited period, and then return him to U.S. military custody, where he would be registered with the International Committee of the Red Cross."

---

112   Mayer: *Dark Side*

113   Tenet, George: *At the Center of the Storm*. New York, HarperCollins, 2007, p. 353.

During the torture sessions described in previous pages by al-Libi's fellow prisoners, al-Libi confessed that Saddam's government had trained al-Qaeda terrorists in the use of chemical and biological weapons – a claim he recanted after being returned to CIA custody in 2004. It was a particularly fraught episode and one that prompted Tenet to reflect in his memoirs:[114]

"Al-Libi's story will no doubt be that he decided to fabricate in order to get better treatment and avoid harsh punishment. He clearly lied. We just don't know when. Did he lie when he first said that al-Qaeda members received training in Iraq or did he lie when he said they did not? In my mind, either case might still be true. Perhaps early on, he was under pressure, assumed his interrogators already knew the story, and sang away. After time passed and it became clear he would not be harmed, he might have changed his story to cloud the mind of his captors."

This troubled statement given by the head of CIA about what al-Libi may or may not have said surely reflects on the unreliability of extracting confessions and information under torture. While al-Libi's cellmates recounted in graphic detail what happened to him, Michael Scheuer, a former CIA agent, is in no doubt al-Libi was tortured, like others sent to other countries.

Although the word of the head of CIA might hold more weight and influence than a random collective of former prisoners of al-Libi, the opinions and thoughts of the former head of the CIA's Osama bin Laden unit should be regarded as credible; Scheuer told me:[115,116]

"We didn't torture anybody and if the practices were torture then the people you go after are the lawyers because everything we did was authorised by eminent Harvard lawyers ... including waterboarding. If you are an intelligence officer in the United States you can barely go down the hall to use the bathroom without a lawyer's approval.

"I developed the rendition programme and when we sent people to countries like Egypt, be in no doubt, everyone knew why they were going there and what was going

---

114   Tenet: *At the Centre of the Storm*, p. 354–355.

115   CIA head of the OBL unit from 1996 to 1999 and also Special Advisor to the Chief of the bin Laden unit from September 2001 to November 2004.

116   He developed the CIA's rendition programme under the Clinton Administration. Interview given to Yvonne Ridley in London in August 2011 following the UK publication of his book.

to happen. They were going to be tortured ... everyone from the President down knew."

Someone else with equally robust opinions is former FBI Agent Ali Soufan, who appeared earlier in this chapter. On September 13 2011, he took part in a documentary called "The Interrogator," which was broadcast on PBS via the American public television's flagship current affairs series Frontline. The author reviewed the transcript, which is available online.[117]Martin Smith's interview with Soufan reveals the reality of the Cairo interrogation and EITs used with al-Libi.

ALI SOUFAN: [behind screen] From my experience, I strongly believe that it is a mistake to use what has become known as enhanced interrogation techniques.

MARTIN SMITH: He appeared, his identity hidden behind a screen, before a Senate committee investigating how and why the Bush White House approved the use of enhanced interrogation techniques.

ALI SOUFAN: These techniques, from an operational perspective, are slow, ineffective, unreliable and harmful to our efforts to defeat al-Qaeda.

MARTIN SMITH: At one point, he alluded to the case of Ibn al Sheikh al Libi ... Al Libi was an al-Qaeda military instructor. When he was captured in Pakistan in 2001, he cooperated at first with FBI interrogators. But with White House permission, the CIA flew him to Egypt for tougher questioning ...

ALI SOUFAN: Ibn Sheikh al Libi, after real macho interrogation – this is enhanced interrogation techniques on steroids – he admitted that al-Qaeda and Saddam were working together. He admitted that al-Qaeda and Saddam were working together on WMDs. That information was given as evidence to Secretary Powell, and Colin Powell went to the U.N. Everybody remembers that speech.

COLIN POWELL, Secretary of State: [at United Nations] I can trace the story of a senior terrorist operative telling how Iraq provided training in these weapons to al-Qaeda –

---

117   Transcript and 28-minute-long video of the Frontline documentary, "The Interrogator." Accessed at http://www.pbs.org/wgbh/pages/frontline/the-interrogator/.

ALI SOUFAN: After we went to Iraq, after we found out that there is [were] no WMDs, after we found out that al-Qaeda and Saddam were not working together, they went back to Ibn Sheikh al Libi – and this is all according to the Armed Services Committee – and they asked him, "Why did you lie?" He said, "Well, I gave you what you want to hear."

MARTIN SMITH: But the consequences of –

ALI SOUFAN: Tragic! Absolutely. The world is different. Look at all the blood that we lost in Iraq. Look about how the Iraq war helped al-Qaeda, both with recruits and financially. It's tragic. Tragic.

The acute pain and embarrassment over the WMD intelligence failure in Iraq is probably felt nowhere more sharply than among Colin Powell[118] and his supporters,[119] including Col. Lawrence Wilkerson, a longtime Powell adviser who served as his chief of staff from 2002 through 2005. He recounted:

"I look back on it, and I still say it was the lowest point in my life … [Powell] came through the door … and he had in his hands a sheaf of papers, and he said, 'This is what I've got to present at the United Nations according to the White House, and you need to look at it.' It was anything but an intelligence document. It was, as some people characterized it later, sort of a Chinese menu from which you could pick and choose."

Again, there appears to be a discrepancy among the shared recollections during the period of the now infamous UN speech made by Powell, especially from Karl Rove's perspective from inside the West Wing of the White House. Curiously, George Tenet's memoirs devote an entire chapter[120] to the intelligence behind Powell's address without making one reference or mention to the al-Libi confession, claiming that Iraqi dictator Saddam Hussein was in league with al-Qaeda. However, he does conclude that "flawed information" was presented to Congress, Bush and the UN, adding that it "should never have happened."

---

118   Retired four-star general in the US military who served in the Bush Administration as Secretary of State from 2001–2005.

119   CNN presents documentary "Dead Wrong – Inside an Intelligence Meltdown." August 23 2005. Online reference: accessed at http://edition.cnn.com/2005/WORLD/meast/08/19/POWell.un/index.html.

120   Tenet, George: *At the Center of the Storm.* New York, Harper Collins, 2007, p. 369–383.

Colin Powell's memoirs[121] are quite blunt about the address he made before the UN; in fact, he devotes an entire chapter to the topic under the simple heading February 5, 2003 The United Nations. Describing it as *"one of the worst intelligence failures in U.S. history,"* he concludes with a determination to ensure that lessons learned are never *"forgotten or ignored."*

Again, even with the benefit of hindsight, it is impossible to judge whether the al-Libi testimony used to substantiate allegations that Saddam was working with al-Qaeda and was prepared to provide it with WMD, triggered the war in Iraq.

Tom Malinowski, the head of Human Rights Watch Washington office, said:[122] *"I would speculate that he was missing because he was such an embarrassment to the Bush administration. He was Exhibit A in the narrative that tortured confessions contributed to the massive intelligence failure that preceded the Iraq war."*

What is clear is that after four intensive days and nights spent in CIA headquarters with key personnel, Powell was convinced that al-Libi's confession would form a key plank of the case for war that he would submit before the United Nations on February 5 2003.

The false confession by al-Libi, given deliberately or otherwise, also had an immediate consequence thousands of miles away in London, where a group of Algerian men were arrested and accused of a mass murder plot involving the manufacture of the poison ricin.[123] The British media front pages carried the news that anti-terror police had disrupted an al-Qaeda cell poised to unleash the deadly poison on the capital. Police had reportedly found traces of ricin, as well as a cache of bomb- and poison-making equipment, in a north London flat. When the case came to trial at the Old Bailey, a very different story emerged, as author and jury member Lawrence Archer explained:[124]

"There was no ricin and no sophisticated plot. Rarely has a legal case been so shamelessly distorted by government, media and security forces to push their own

121   Powell, Colin: *It Worked for Me.* New York, Harper Collins, 2012, p. 217–224.

122   Finn, Peter: "Detainee Who Gave False Iraq Data Dies in Prison." *The Washington Post.* World Pages, May 12 2009.

123   Archer, Lawrence and Bawdon, Fiona: *Ricin! The Inside Story of the Terror Plot That Never Was.* London, Pluto Press, 2010.

124   The author interviewed Lawrence Archer at his book launch in 2010. Archer had the rare distinction of being a serving member on the so-called "ricin jury" as well as the author.

'tough on terror' agendas. In the meantime, those Algerian men spent three years in a maximum security prison on remand for a crime that did not exist, that had come from faulty intelligence from a man tortured out of his mind."

His co-author Fiona Bawdon, also interviewed at the book's media launch, told me:

"It emerged during the trial that just two days after the dramatic police raid – and the day before news of the ricin find made the headlines – it had been established no ricin had been found. A few weeks later, in February, the US Secretary of State, Colin Powell, said in a speech to the UN Security Council seeking its support for war on Iraq that the London ricin find was evidence of the 'sinister nexus' between Al-Qaeda and Saddam Hussein's regime. It has never been explained how the initial false positive result was passed on to the media as fact. Nor is it clear why it took the scientists at Porton Down a further three months to tell the police or government that there was no ricin, after all."

No clues appear in either Blair's or Powell's memoirs – neither man recalls or refers to the so-called Ricin Plot, nor do they refer to the case of Ibn Sheikh al-Libi, whose false confessions went on to spawn panic and alarm among ordinary Londoners. Did al-Libi deliberately make up the story to cause mass panic or was he, as has been suggested, inventing a plot to please his tormentors in Cairo? There can never be a convincing answer because the one person who knows the truth is dead. Al-Libi's body was found hanging in his cell in Abu Salim Prison in May 2009.

While the Gaddafi regime was keen to promote the idea al-Libi had killed himself, a subsequent interview I did inside a heavily guarded prison in Zawiya revealed a different story. A former guard turned prisoner told me he had found Ibn Sheikh's body the next morning and that he had been killed by the regime. The interview was given freely and the prisoner did not appear to be under any duress to see or speak with me.

But what I also established was that British intelligence was intrigued by al-Libi and had interviewed him, not only while he was held in Guantanamo, but during his US rendition programme which took him to a secure unit in Morocco. In statements from both his family and former cellmate Sheikh Mohamed Bosidra, they confirmed that he told them he had spoken with SIS several times and one time the British agents even informed him they had intercepted his wife's phone calls.

"They told him his daughter was learning to talk and talk. They were trying to ingratiate themselves with him by updating him on his family's progress. She was living in Syria at the time before the start of the Arab Spring when they eavesdropped on her calls," Sheikh Bosidra told me.

This is of particular significance since the UK Government has always insisted its intelligence services were never compromised or complicit in the US torture and rendition programmes. However it has now emerged through an article in The Guardian in May 2016 that Eliza Manningham-Buller banned MI6 officers from working in MI5's headquarters when she learned of the full extent of the involvement of British spies and Libyan dissidents. The former Director General even wrote to the then Prime Minister Tony Blair to complain about the behaviour of MI6 agents[125].

Perhaps this episode is best summed up by Rand Beers in an article[126] he wrote a year before he was appointed as Under Secretary of Homeland Security by President Barack Obama on June 19 2009. He said:

"Of all of the pieces of intelligence assembled in the lead-up to war, this one was the most chilling: the prospect of weapons of mass destruction, including nuclear weapons, under Osama bin Ladin's control. And so we went to war to prevent this nightmare from occurring. What better proof that torture works?

"But in January 2004, al-Libi recanted his confession. He said that he had invented the information because he was afraid of being further abused by his interrogators. The CIA withdrew the intelligence. It has since emerged that some U.S. intelligence agencies doubted al-Libi's claims from the very beginning. The administration's best case for the value of enhanced interrogation techniques, then, turned out to have been fundamentally flawed. If the consequences of torture are as catastrophic as embarking upon the Iraq War on the basis of fabricated information, it emasculates the claims by torture's defenders that the practice saves lives."

---

125   The Guardian newspaper report: http://www.theguardian.com/uk-news/2016/may/31/ revealed-britain-rendition-policy-rift-between-spy-agencies-mi6-mi5
126   Beers, Rand: "No Torture, No Exceptions." *Washington Monthly*, January/February/March 2008, accessed at http://www.washingtonmonthly.com/features/2008/0801.beers.html.

7
Conclusion and Final Thoughts

The issue of the use of torture was raised during the French-Algerian and Vietnam conflicts but the anger and polarisation it has created since 9/11 – a day which has become an indelible stain on the American memory and psyche[1] – continues to rage unabated in the 21st century. However, while passions run high over the rights and wrongs of its deployment, few have asked the question of how effective it is as a weapon in modern warfare, when conventional armies are being forced to confront the challenges of new types of battlefields.

Although America's secret rendition programme had already been launched by the previous Clinton Administration, in which terror suspects were sent by the CIA to other countries to be tortured, September 11 2001 marked a turning point in the way the US would handle enemies of the state.

The military term – "enemy combatant" – was reinvented to label terror suspects, and EITs were developed as part of the GWOT, including a conscious decision to bypass international laws as set out in the Geneva Conventions. As previously discussed, the Bush Administration argued that the GWOT was not a conventional war, nor was al-Qaeda and/or the Taliban a formal military entity.

While the rights and wrongs are still being forensically scrutinised and debated by lawmakers and human rights groups more than a decade on, very little has been said about the effectiveness of torture or how that effectiveness can be measured in terms of success.

The GWOT has no conventional battlefield, and America's enemies, presented as followers of extreme brands of Islam, wear no uniform, nor do they fight under one nation or flag. Like many terrorist organisations, al-Qaeda and its followers commit atrocities on civilian populations or fight in situations in which innocent civilians and bystanders are exposed and endangered.

---

1   Marist College Institute for Public Opinion: NY1 – Marist Poll. September 6 2011 found 97 percent of New Yorkers recalled what they were doing on 9/11.

Thus, it is fair to conclude that conventional – even sophisticated – weaponry and warfare can not combat this new enemy which confronts the USA and its NATO allies on many different levels and in many different guises. As a result, in any counter-insurgency operation, human intelligence takes on a greater significance with the specific aim to undermine, outwit and ultimately defeat a small but resilient enemy.

But just how far is the US prepared to go in this asymmetric war and, by using torture, how much is it prepared to sacrifice in civil liberties and freedoms to attain a military win before there is a loss in political terms as the public appetite for victory wanes in favour of compromise or even partial surrender?

The most senior members of the Bush Administration, including the US President himself, endorsed the use of EITs, justifying their use with the argument of the volonté générale or general will based on the theories of Jean-Jacques Rousseau.

Harvard lawyer Alan Dershowitz and several members of the US intelligence community, from the CIA director down, chose to cite the "ticking bomb" scenario as further justification for the implementation of torture, with Dershowitz submitting a strong argument for the use of special warrants which would make legal the execution of torture by US intelligence agents.

Dershowitz justifies the use of torture by saying it could save an "enormous number of lives," adding that terror suspects are unlikely to volunteer information on this scale unless extreme measures of pressure are implemented – that is, torture.

Yet, as mentioned in the previous chapter, Rand Beers, a former counter-terrorism adviser on the National Security Council, hinted at the deaths of hundreds of thousands of Iraqi innocents due to the flawed intelligence produced from the torture interrogations of Ibn Sheikh al Libi, which set in motion the invasion of Iraq.

Without exception, all of those mentioned in this book who promoted and endorsed the use of EITs, including waterboarding (later to be deemed torture by the Obama Administration), used the backdrop of 9/11 as a reminder to both the general public and critics of the possible outcomes of future intelligence failures.

With the possible complicit support of Hollywood, it is no coincidence that the age-old theme of the ticking bomb scenario began to re-emerge and present itself in major TV series and movies soon after 9/11. Could this surreptitious use of popular media be responsible for embedding in the public psyche a feeling of acceptance of the need to torture terrorist suspects for the common good?

Perhaps it is still too early to draw any conclusions on the use of media, but by stark comparison, the French population demanded an end to the occupation of Algeria by the French armed forces when it emerged that the French military had implemented torture against the resistance movements on a massive scale.

Not only did the French military fail to win the Algerian war, but France lost a strategic territory largely because of pressure brought to bear on its politicians as growing public opinion demanded a political solution and compromise. It could be argued that once it became public knowledge, the use of torture turned out to be a spectacular failure in the 1954–62 campaign, despite the insistence of senior military officials – including Generals Paul Aussaresses and Marcel Bigeard – that it was an essential weapon in COIN operations.

Although various US generals have expressed their admiration for the COIN techniques employed by their French counterparts during the Algerian war, it is worth remembering the caution cited previously in this book, from the US Army Field Manual 3-24 on COIN, which states:[2]

> *"This official condoning of torture on the part of French Army leadership had several negative consequences. It empowered the moral legitimacy of the opposition, undermined the French moral legitimacy, and caused internal fragmentation among serving officers that led to an unsuccessful coup attempt in 1962. In the end, failure to comply with moral and legal restrictions against torture severely undermined French efforts and contributed to their loss despite several significant military victories."*

As discussed in Chapter 3, this critical observation tends to conflict with the decision-making process in the Bush Administration, which led directly to the use of EITs. So quite how members of this administration would define success to justify its use is not explained in their books or media interviews, although in their defence, they have argued that success is difficult to measure because many intelligence operations which prevent terrorist attacks are covert and classified, and therefore both the media and public are generally unaware of them.

---

2   *US Army Field Manual 3-24: Counterinsurgency*, p. 252.

However, a chilling observation once used by the Provisional Irish Republican Army[3] (IRA) is quoted or paraphrased by COIN exponents as a reminder of how close are the margins between success and failure in terms of combatting terrorism. Following its failure to assassinate the British Prime Minister Margaret Thatcher the IRA issued this statement:[4]

"Mrs. Thatcher will now realise that Britain cannot occupy our country and torture our prisoners and shoot our people in their own streets and get away with it. Today we were unlucky, but remember we only have to be lucky once. You will have to be lucky always. Give Ireland peace and there will be no more war."

It was a theme picked up by George W Bush in 2004 during his first presidential debate with Senator John Kerry, when he said: *"You know, we have to be right 100 percent of the time. And the enemy only has to be right once to hurt us."*[5]

In other words, the Bush Administration was prepared to do whatever it felt necessary to prevent another terrorist hit on its own territory. In his memoirs, Bush explains that 9/11 had a wider effect on the US which would impact the country for years to come:[6]

"The toll of 9/11 will always be measured by the 2,973 lives stolen and many others devastated. But the economic cost was shattering as well. The New York Stock Exchange shut down for four days, the longest suspension of trading since the Great Depression. When the markets reopened, the Dow Jones plunged 684 points, the biggest single-day drop in history – to that point.

"The impact of the attacks rippled throughout the economy. Tourism plummeted. Several airlines filed for bankruptcy. Many restaurants sat virtually empty. Some hotels reported business being down as much as 90 percent. Manufacturers and small businesses laid off workers as skittish buyers cancelled their orders. By the end of the year, more than a million Americans had lost their jobs. 'The United States and the

---

3   Irish revolutionary paramilitary organisation.

4   Taylor, Peter: *Brits: The War Against the IRA*. London, Bloomsbury Publishing, 2001, p. 265.

5   Transcript of First Presidential televised debate on September 30 2003 in Florida and published online in *The Washington Post*. Accessed at http://www.washingtonpost.com/wp-srv/politics/debatereferee/debate_0930.html.

6   Bush: *Decision Points*, p. 443.

rest of the world are likely to experience a full-blown recession now,' one economist predicted.

"That was what the terrorists intended. 'Al Qaeda spent $500,000 on the event,' Osama bin Ladin later bragged, 'while America ... lost – according to the lowest estimate – $500 billion.'"

Unable to contemplate more deaths on such a large scale, as well as suffering the potential fall-out financially and politically from another terrorist strike, it is therefore understandable why the pro-active – bordering on aggressive – reaction of the Bush Administration followed; some of the closest US allies, including British Prime Minister Tony Blair, added their support, pointing out that the *"rules of the game have changed."*

However, the former head of MI5, Eliza Manningham-Buller, who served under Blair, expresses reservations:[7]

"Torture is illegal in our national law and in international law. It is wrong and it is never justified. It is a sadness, and worse, that the previous government of our great ally, the United States, chose to waterboard some detainees. The argument that life-saving intelligence was thereby obtained, and I accept it was, still does not justify it. Torture should be utterly rejected even when it may offer the prospect of saving lives.

"I believe that the acquisition of short-term gain through waterboarding and other forms of mistreatment was a profound mistake and lost the United States moral authority and some of the widespread sympathy it had enjoyed as a result of 9/11. I am confident that I know the answer to the question of whether torture has made the world a safer place. It hasn't."

Despite the groundswell of opinion elsewhere in the world, the American public does not appear to be in a hurry to make human rights and the so-called torture debate a priority election or political issue; until it does, it seems unlikely that subsequent US administrations will want to dilute certain COIN activities in the GWOT deemed outside of international law.

---

7   Manningham-Buller, *Securing Freedom*, p. 48–49.

However, that is not one of the main concerns of critics regarding the use of torture. In Chapter 6, some of the surviving victims of torture express their opinions and recall their own experiences, in which they highlight the following concerns: 1) torture victims will invent stories to please their interrogator; 2) intelligence given under duress is unreliable; 3) interrogations then become based on invented plots; and 4) flawed intelligence leads to political and military errors of judgement, perhaps the worst example being the invasion of Iraq.

Last, but not least, is an aspect of torture not always commented on, and that is claims that some victims may have been radicalised into joining the GWOT. There is certainly evidence to show that a number of terror suspects have joined or perhaps even rejoined the asymmetric battlefield to wage war against the US and its allies. Others have joined in fighting in Afghanistan, Pakistan, Libya, Iraq, Yemen and other fields of conflict.

Included in the first witness accounts in this book are personal views by the late journalist Christopher Hitchens, who submitted himself to waterboarding to experience firsthand this specific form of torture, and US Senator John McCain, a Vietnam veteran and former POW, who endured torture during his captivity.

Few will forget McCain's powerful testimony on the floor of the Senate just before the release of the 500-page summary on CIA Torture indicating that torture is unreliable. It is worth recounting this passage: "*What might come as a surprise, not just to our enemies, but to many Americans, is how little these practices did to aid our efforts to bring 9/11 culprits to justice and to find and prevent terrorist attacks today and tomorrow. That could be a real surprise, since it contradicts the many assurances provided by intelligence officials on the record and in private that enhanced interrogation techniques were indispensable in the war against terrorism. And I suspect the objection of those same officials to the release of this report is really focused on that disclosure – torture's ineffectiveness – because we gave up much in the expectation that torture would make us safe. Too much.*"

While the ex-Guantanamo detainees, members of the former LIFG and other dissident groups could have an axe to grind, both Hitchens and McCain could not be accused of anti-American bias. However, their fears over the use of torture echoed the same sentiments.

Both feared torture could be used by other regimes on US captives and thus expose Americans travelling overseas to potential dangers. In the same vein, they felt that the ill-treatment of enemy prisoners could endanger US troops, who may themselves become POWs. These fears were extended beyond the GWOT, predicting a possible legacy of torturing American POWs in future conflicts.

McCain also dispelled the myth that the use of torture led to the demise of Osama bin Laden during the Obama Administration and other successful intelligence-led operations, as claimed by members of the Bush Administration, including the former US president himself.

There may be additional negative fallout from the deployment of torture which may very well reveal itself during any future military trial of KSM. His credibility as a reliable witness falls into question because he was waterboarded 183 times, according to now-declassified documents.

However, because the Obama Administration is determined to put KSM on trial, possibly to prove to the world that the US still believes in the concept of a judicial process for terror suspects, it will give rise to the very sort of platform which COIN expert and self-confessed torturer Lieutenant Colonel David Galula warned against in his book on counter-insurgency warfare.

This particular passage, stated by Galula in Chapter 5, could even serve as a cautionary warning over the decision to try KSM who, since his capture, torture and detention, has gained international notoriety:[8]

> *"The arrested insurgent can count almost automatically on some support from the legitimate opposition parties and groups. Referred to the courts, he will take refuge in chicanery and exploit to the utmost every advantage provided by the existing laws. Worse yet, the trial itself will serve as a sounding board for his cause."*

It is quite clear from the observations of co-authors Terry McDermott and Josh Meyer[9] that the prospect of a high-profile trial of KSM highlights Galula's greatest concerns regarding publicity by and about terror suspects. McDermott and Meyer say they also believe KSM continues to pose a threat, despite his ongoing detention in GTMO.

---

8   Galula: *Counterinsurgency Warfare*, p. 45.
9   McDermott and Meyer: *KSM*, p. 286–287.

"In a way, bin Ladin's death, though celebrated, was inconsequential ... By contrast, even years after his capture, KSM remained a threat ... Through his aura of invincibility, through ghosts such as Shukrijumah,[10] KSM has retained his power, his ability to strike fear into the hearts of potential victims, which is the first goal of all terrorism. Caged in one of the highest-security prisons ever built – a prison within a prison within a military base on a remote island – he endured, through his network, his legacy, through ideas he had already given to others, as a threat. KSM, years after he was last able to issue a single order, remained, in some real sense, in command."

The controversial decision by the Bush Administration regarding the authorisation given to waterboard KSM could prove to be a serious own goal, since the publicity surrounding the al-Qaeda suspect's torture has generated a great deal of propaganda, spawned international debates and raised his profile around the world.

Had he gone through a conventional judicial process, without torture, when he was captured in March 2003, one wonders if his name would be as instantly recognised a decade later, which has served only to increase his status and his cause among the global jihadist movements of today.

David Z Nevin, Khaled Sheikh Mohammed's lead lawyer, provides a cogent view of the implications of his client's case for the US.

"I think you're asking the wrong question in terms of does torture work. It's a bit like asking if slavery works, and the truth is it worked very well for some but it was still wrong.

"There's a reason that nations of the world came together to outlaw torture, just as those same nations outlawed slavery and genocide. This kind of behaviour is abhorrent to humanity. The government claims that when Khaled Sheikh Mohammed was arrested, they believed a follow-on attack from 9/11 was imminent and they wanted information on that.

---

10   Saudi-born Adnan Gulshair el Shukrijumah is listed on the FBI's website as a "most wanted." As KSM's replacement as chief of al-Qaeda's external operations council, his responsibility is said to include planning attacks outside of Afghanistan. Accessed at http://www.fbi.gov/wanted/wanted_terrorists/adnan-g.-el-shukrijumah/.

"The Conventions Against Torture recognize that in the heat and fear of battle there might be a tendency to say 'let's do it anyway.' The nations of the world realised this and agreed it should never happen under any circumstances – torture is a practice which is universally reviled. There are some practices like slavery and genocide that are reviled, and torture is another one. It is unspeakable at all times, even – or perhaps especially – when the chips are down.

"We know that torture and trauma have dramatic impacts on peoples' personalities, and the torture programme used was specifically designed to disrupt the personalities and to achieve total compliance so victims stopped thinking for themselves. As with Mr. Mohammed, we know this has had a dramatic impact on his personality and he suffers from post-traumatic stress disorder – all the detainees do.

"This is a terrible situation and the truth is it produced no useful intelligence despite claims made by the pro-torture lobby. It has been said that Mr. Mohammed gave information which led to the arrest of a certain person, but on investigation that person had already been arrested and was already in custody. There is no evidence that Mr. Mohammed said anything useful as a result of being tortured.

"I've spent a career as a lawyer and if someone told me 13 years ago that we would be representing a client who'd been tortured for three and a half years incommunicado we would have said 'not in the USA.' No way.

"We are not talking about a rogue police officer who drags a prisoner out of his cell in the middle of the night to harm him. We are talking about conscious decisions made at the highest level – made in the White House.

"Alan Dershowitz talked about torture warrants and I don't ever see them becoming consistent with US law. We know the Convention Against Torture makes torture an international crime and you can't escape that. But by using terms like EIT instead of torture and doing it in secret ... you can't rule anything out."

It is not without some irony to note, however, that while the Obama Administration outlawed the use of waterboarding and other EITs, calling the methods torture, it has now attracted international criticism for choosing instead to eliminate terror suspects by the use of unmanned, remote-controlled aircraft called drones[11] in the

---

11   On June 20 2012, China and Russia jointly issued a statement at the UN Human Rights
        Council, backed by other countries, condemning drone attacks.

conflict zones of Afghanistan, Pakistan, Yemen, Syria, Iraq and Somalia. Accused of doing away with the concept of a trial by jury, this new method has drawn a massive public outcry from human rights groups[12] – but it is fair to assume that it would meet the approval of another COIN expert and theorist, the late Colonel Roger Trinquier, mentioned several times in Chapter 5 regarding his robust criticism of conventional armies' abilities to adapt to modern warfare.

Victory over terrorism in modern warfare means only one thing in his view, as outlined here:[13]

"In seeking a solution, it is essential to realize that in modern warfare we are not up against just a few armed bands spread across a given territory, but rather against an armed clandestine organization whose essential role is to impose its will upon the population. Victory will be obtained only through the complete destruction of that organization. This is the master concept that must guide us in our study of modern warfare."

Of course, students and experts on the philosophy of military theorist Major General Carl Philipp Gottfried von Clausewitz[14] will recognise echoes of his work in Trinquier's writings. Clausewitz is credited with perceiving war as a political, social and military phenomenon which might – depending on the political climate – draw in the entire population of a nation at war in attempting to impose a government's policies and will upon the enemy.

However, far from imposing its will on an entire nation, (or in this case the West) what has emerged from this research for this book is the polarisation of those who fall largely into two schools of thought – some who believe in the use of torture to save the lives of innocents and others who believe its deployment is harmful and

---

12   Christof Heyns, the UN special rapporteur on extrajudicial killings, summary or arbitrary executions, attended a conference in Geneva on June 20 2012 where he said that President Obama's attacks would encourage others to flout international law. At the conference, organised by the ACLU, he also suggested that some of the attacks could constitute war crimes. Ref: Bowcott, Owen: "Drone Strikes Threaten 50 Years of International Law, Says UN Rapporteur." The Guardian, World News Section, June 22 2012.

13   Trinquier: *Modern Warfare*, p. 7.

14   Born 1780–1831, Prussian soldier best known as a military theorist and author with a specific focus on the philosophical examination of war in all its aspects. His work is still considered relevant today, with more than a dozen English-language books focusing on him in last decade. For more, read: Clausewitz, Von Carl: *On War*. Edited and translated by Michael Eliot Howard. Chichester, Princeton University Press, 1976.

will cost the lives of innocents because of the poor-quality and often misleading intelligence gained.

The first group expects instant results while the latter fears the negative, long-term consequences of breaking international law. In all of the books read, statements taken, eye witness accounts recorded and documents scrutinised, during the research for this book, one individual emerges as probably the most powerful advocate against the use of torture as a weapon in modern warfare ... and that person is American patriot and decorated war hero, Republican Senator John McCain.

His harrowing personal account,[15] covering 33 pages in the book Reporting Vietnam, leaves no doubt as to the validity of the testimony of someone who has experienced the pain and trauma of being tortured into making a false confession. In addition, McCain is a third-generation military man who was proud to serve his country in uniform before going on to become a long-serving Senator and US Presidential candidate.

Drawing on his experiences as a POW, victim of torture, US Naval Lieutenant Commander and a veteran American politician, McCain wrote a powerful editorial,[16] which provides a worthy conclusion to this research on the effectiveness of torture as a weapon in modern warfare.

"I know those who approved and employed these practices were dedicated to protecting Americans. I know they were determined to keep faith with the victims of terrorism and to prove to our enemies that the United States would pursue justice relentlessly no matter how long it took ... I know from personal experience that the abuse of prisoners sometimes produces good intelligence but often produces bad intelligence because under torture a person will say anything he thinks his captors want to hear — true or false — if he believes it will relieve his suffering. Often, information provided to stop the torture is deliberately misleading.

"Mistreatment of enemy prisoners endangers our own troops, who might someday be held captive. While some enemies, and al-Qaeda surely, will never be bound by the principle of reciprocity, we should have concern for those Americans captured by more conventional enemies, if not in this war then in the next.

---

15   McCain: in Bates, Milton J: *Reporting Vietnam*, p. 434–463.
16   McCain, John: "Bin Ladin's Death and the Debate over Torture." *The Washington Post*, Opinion page, May 12 2011.

"As we debate how the United States can best influence the course of the Arab Spring, can't we all agree that the most obvious thing we can do is stand as an example of a nation that holds an individual's human rights as superior to the will of the majority or the wishes of government? Individuals might forfeit their life as punishment for breaking laws, but even then, as recognized in our Constitution's prohibition of cruel and unusual punishment, they are still entitled to respect for their basic human dignity, even if they have denied that respect to others."

Moral and legal issues aside, it is quite obvious torture produces unreliable intelligence and is about as effective a weapon in modern warfare as a substandard Thompson submachine gun would have been for a soldier embattled on the front-line during the Second World War.

However, intelligence is crucial when combating terrorism or asymmetric warfare, and while insurgency is relatively cheap, counter-insurgency is not. The Western military, especially in the US, is constantly being thrown different challenges by the rapidly changing political landscape of the Muslim world. Unless it adapts to new methods in COIN operations, resorting to old tactics like torture will prove to be useless in the face of the new, ruthless threat posed by 21st century insurgents.

Glossary of Terms

ACLU: American Civil Liberties Union
AFM: Army Field Manual
AFP: Agence France-Presse
AG: Attorney General
AI: Amnesty International
ANO: Abu Nidal Organisation
AQAP: al-Qaeda in the Arabian Peninsula
AUMF: Authorization for Use of Military Force
CGS: Committee of General Security
CIA: Central Intelligence Agency
CINC: Commander in Chief
COIN: Counter Insurgency
CSI: Center for the Study of Intelligence
CTU: Counter Terrorist Unit
Daesh: aka Islamic State of Iraq and the Levant
DoD: Department of Defence
EIT: Enhanced Interrogation Techniques
FBI: Federal Bureau of Investigation
FFF: Free French Forces
FLN: National Liberation Front
FM: Field Manual
FOIA: Freedom of Information Act
GTMO: Guantanamo Bay Naval Base
GWOT: Global War on Terror
HRW: Human Rights Watch
HVD: High-Value Detainees
ICC: International Criminal Court
ICRC: International Committee of the Red Cross
IRA: Provisional Irish Republican Army
ISAF: International Security Assistance Force
ISIL/ISIS: Islamic State of Iraq and the Levant, alternatively translated as Islamic
    State of Iraq and Syria or Islamic State of Iraq and al-Sham or Daesh
JTF-GTMO: Joint Task Force Guantanamo
JSOC: Joint Special Operations Command
KLFCW: Kuala Lumpur Foundation to Criminalise War
KLWCC: Kuala Lumpur War Crimes Commission
KLWCT: Kuala Lumpur War Crimes Tribunal
KSM: Khalid Sheikh Mohammed
LIFG: Libyan Islamic Fighting Group
NATO: North Atlantic Treaty Organisation
NGO: Non-Governmental Organisation
NSA: National Security Adviser

NSC: National Security Council
OBL: Osama bin Laden
ODNI: Office of the Director of National Intelligence
OLC: Office of Legal Counsel
POW: Prisoner of War
PRO: Public Records Office
SAM: Surface to Air Missile
SDECE: External Documentation and Counter-Espionage Service
SERE: Survival, Evasion, Resistance and Escape
SJC: Senate Judiciary Committee
SSI: Strategic Studies Institute
STOP: Stop Torture Permanently
TSCTI: Trans-Saharan Counterterrorism Initiative
UN: United Nations
UNCAT: United Nations Convention Against Torture
USFOR-A: US Forces Afghanistan
WHO: World Health Organisation
WMA: World Medical Association
WMD: Weapons of Mass Destruction

BIBLIOGRAPHY

PRIMARY SOURCES: Unpublished

Official documents

The National Archives: Dusko Popov, WWII double agent TRICYCLE (KV 2/845-866, *see also* double agent Ivan Popov, KV 2/867-870)

Interviews

Aamer, Shaker: Ex-GTMO detainee; in London, January 20 2016.

Abassi, Feroz: Ex-GTMO detainee; in London, via email February 2012.

Al Saadi, Sami: Ex-LIFG; in person, recorded by video at hotel Tripoli, Libya, May 2012.

Amerine, Jason: Lt Col US Special Forces; via email, Nov 24 2015.

Arar, Maher: Canadian-based former US rendition and Syrian torture victim; via email, August 2012.

Begg, Moazzam: Ex-GTMO detainee and Director of Cageprisoners NGO; on video, by email and in person, February 2012.

Belhaj, Abdul Hakim: Ex-Abu Salim Prison and ex-LIFG; on video and in person Tripoli, Libya, May 2012.

Bosidra, Sheikh Mohamed: Ex-Abu Salim prisoner; Benghazi, April 2011.

Derghoul, Tarek: Ex-GTMO detainee; in London, via email, February 2012.

Doyle, Professor Francis: International human rights lawyer; in person in Kuala Lumpur, May 2012.

Granger, Montgomery J, Major (Ret.): Ex-GTMO medic; guard and author via email, September 2012

Mohamad, Mahathir: Ex-PM of Malaysia; in person in Kuala Lumpur, May 2012.

Peirce, Gareth: International human rights lawyer; in person, London office and Tripoli hotel, May 2012.

Rebaii, Mohamed: Misrata rebel commander and ex-LIFG; in person and video at home Misrata, Libya, May 2012.

PRIMARY SOURCES: Published

Camp 020: MI5 and the Nazi Spies. British Public Record Office, 2000.

Custody, February 2007 – An exact replica of the leaked report: http://www.nybooks.com/media/doc/2010/04/22/icrc-report.pdf.

Hansard, Column 752: Guantanamo Civil Litigation Settlement, November 16 2010.

Verbatim Transcript of Combatant Status Review Tribunal Hearing for ISM 10025, March 10 2007 – Unclassified.

ICRC report on the Treatment of the Fourteen "High-Value Detainees" in CIA. Custody (February 2007) – An exact replica of the leaked report, accessed at http://www.nybooks.com/media/doc/2010/04/22/icrc-report.pdf.

Prime Minister of Canada Stephen Harper's Office. Press release headed: Prime Minister releases letter of apology to Maher Arar and his family and announces completion of mediation process. January 26 2007, Ottawa, Ontario.

Archives: US Presidential Speeches & Executive Order – The Scripps Library, The Miller Center, University of Virginia

Bush, George W, "Authorization for Use of Military Force (AUMF)," passed on September 18 2001.

Bush, George W, Speech before a Joint Session of Congress, September 20 2001 (Washington).

Bush, George W, "Detention, Treatment, and Trial of Certain Non-Citizens in the War Against Terrorism," Military Order passed on November 13 2001.

Obama, Barack, Executive Order 13491 – "Ensuring Lawful Interrogations," January 22 2009.

Obama, Barack, Statement issued from White House press office, April 16 2009, informing that the Department of Justice will release certain memos issued by the OLC between 2002 and 2005, outlining techniques that were used in the interrogation of terrorism suspects during that period.

Archives: US Justice Department Office of Legal Counsel

Standards of Conduct for Interrogation under 18 U.S.C. sections 2340-2340A
1.1.1 Part I
1.1.2 Part II
1.1.3 Part III
1.1.4 Part IV
1.1.5 Part V
1.1.6 Part VI
1.1.7 Conclusion
1.2 Interrogation of al-Qaeda operative
1.2.1 Part I
1.2.2 Part II
1.2.3 Part III
1.2.4 Conclusion
1.3 Letter from John Yoo to Alberto Gonzales
1.3.1 Part I
1.3.2 Part II
1.3.3 Part III
1.3.4 Conclusion

* The Office of Legal Counsel opinions can be found on the OLC website at http://www.justice.gov/olc/ for the years 1992 to the present by using keyword searches. The above list comprises references to the so-called "Torture Memos," otherwise known as "Standards of Conduct for Interrogation under 18 U.S.C. sections 2340-2340A," "Interrogation of al-Qaeda" and an untitled letter from legal advisers, including then US Attorney General, Alberto Gonzales; the Assistant Attorney General, Jay Bybee and a former official in the US States Department of Justice, John Choon Yoo, from January 2002 through to 2009.

US DoJ, OLC May 30 2005. 0000011 Application of United States Obligations Under Article 16 of the Convention Against Torture to Certain Techniques that May Be Used in the Interrogation of High Value al Qaeda Detainees.

UN Press releases: "Pillay Deeply Disturbed by US Failure to Close Guantanamo Prison." Press release issued January 23 2012 from the Office of the High Commissioner for Human Rights.

Official publications

Amnesty International. Torture in the Eighties. USA Edition. Amnesty International Publication, 1973.

Committee on Armed Services, United States Senate. Report on Inquiry into the Treatment of Detainees in U.S. Custody November 20 2008 and declassified in April 2009.

Counterinsurgency. US Army Field Manual 3-24 and US Marine Corps Warfighting Publication. No 3-33.5. Washington, December 2006.

Geneva Conventions.

George W Bush v The US Constitution. "The Downing Street Memos and Deception, Manipulation, Torture, Retribution, Coverups in the Iraq War and Illegal Domestic Spying." Compiled by the House Judiciary Committee Democratic Staff. Academy Chicago Publishers, 2006.

Hague Conventions.

Nuremberg Charter.

UN Convention Against Torture, Article 1.1 United Nations, December 10 1984

United Nations, Treaty Series, vol. 1465, p. 85.

UN, Universal Declaration of Human Rights, Article 5, adopted by the UN General Assembly, Paris, December 10 1948.

The US Army Marine Corps Counterinsurgency Field Manual. University of Chicago Press, 2007.

US Senate Select Committee on Intelligence; Confirmation Hearing for General David H Petraeus, June 23 2011.

WHO report: "The Health Hazards of Organised Violence." Veldhoven, April 22–25 1986.

WMA Declaration of Tokyo, Section 5, October 1975.

Published diaries and memoirs

Blair, Tony: A Journey. London, Arrow Books, 2010.

Bush, George W: Decision Points. London, Virgin Books, 2010.

Cheney, Dick: In My Time. Threshold, August 2011.

Clarke, Richard A: Against All Enemies: Inside America's War on Terror. New York Free Press, 2004.

Gadaffi, Muammar: My Vision. London, John Blake Publishing, 2005.

Kiriakou, John: The Reluctant Spy: My Secret Life in the CIA's War on Terror, New York, Bantam Books, 2009.

Mohamad, Mahathir: A Doctor in the House. The Memoirs of Tun Dr Mahathir Mohamad. Malaysia, MPA Publishing, 2011.

Powell, Colin: It Worked For Me. New York, HarperCollins, 2012.

Powell, Colin: A Soldier's Way. London, Hutchinson, 1995.

Rice, Condoleezza: No Higher Honour. Simon & Schuster UK Ltd., 2011.

Rove, Karl: Courage and Consequence: My Life as a Conservative in the Fight. Simon and Schuster, 2010.

Rumsfeld, Donald: Known and Unknown, A Memoir. New York, Sentinel, 2011.

Tenet, George: At the Center of the Storm. HarperCollins, 2007.

Newspapers and journals

An Awkward Case: Why A Retired General's Admission about Torture in Algeria is Embarassing. The Economist, December 1 2001.

Anderson, Bruce: "We Not Only Have a Right to Use Torture. We Have a Duty." The Independent, London, February 15 2010.

Anthony, Andrew: The Big Showdown. The Observer, September 18 2005.

AP: "Ex-GTMO Detainee and Key Al-Qaeda Organizer Killed in Afghanistan." September 3 2011, accessed at http://www.dailymail.co.uk/news/article-2033254/Ex-GTMO-detainee-killed-Afghanistan.html.

Beach, Bennet H and Yang, John E : The Lawyer of Last Resort. Time Magazine, May 17 1982.

Beers, Rand: No Torture, No Exceptions. Washington Monthly, Jan/Feb/March 2008.

Bernstein, Richard: Kidnapping Has Germans Debating Police Torture. New York Times, April 10 2003.

Campbell, Duncan: "The Ricin Ring that Never Was." The Guardian, April 14 2005.

Carter, Jimmy: A Cruel and Unusual Record. New York Times, June 24 2012, Opinion pages.

Cobain, Ian: Rendition Report that Raises New Questions about Secret Trials. The Guardian, April 9 2012.

Daily Mirror front page showing a skull and crossbones against a map of Britain on its Wednesday front page under the headline "It's Here." January 8 2003.

Drogin, Bob and Miller, Greg: "Spy Agencies Facing Questions of Tactics." Los Angeles Times, October 28 2001.

Editorial: "The Torture Candidates." New York Times, November 15 2011.

Finn, Peter: "Detainee Who Gave False Iraq Data Dies in Libya." Washington Post, May 12 2009.

Fisk, Robert: Rahimullah Yusufzai. Independent on Sunday, March 23 2010.

Henley, Jon: Want to Know if Waterboarding is Torture? Ask Christopher Hitchens. The Guardian July 2 2008 G2 section

Hitchens, Christopher: "Believe Me, It's Torture." Vanity Fair, New York. August 2008.

Hochschild, Adam: What's in a Word? Torture. New York Times, May 23 2004, Opinion pages

James, Barry: General's Confessions of Torture Stun France. New York Times May 5 2001 International pages

MacAskill, Ewan and Hirsch, Afua: "George Bush Calls Off Trip to Switzerland." The Guardian, February 7 2011.

Mazzetti, Mark and Shane, Scott: "Interrogation Memos Detail Harsh Tactics by the CIA." New York Times, April 16 2009.

McCain, John: Bin Laden's Death and the Debate over Torture. Washington Post, May 12 2011, Opinion pages

McCoy, Alfred W: "The Myth of the Ticking Time Bomb." The Progressive, October 2006.

Miller, Greg: John Rizzo: "The Most Influential Career Lawyer in CIA History." Los Angeles Times, June 29 2009.

Mukasey, Michael B: The Waterboarding Trail to Bin Ladin , The Wall Street Journal, May 6 2011 Opinion pages

Norton-Taylor, Richard: "Straw, MI6 and Libyan Renditions: An Issue that Will Not Go Away." The Guardian, April 18 2012.

Norton-Taylor, Richard: "Guantanamo: Security Services Must Be Protected, Says Ken Clarke." The Guardian, November 17 2010.

Norton-Taylor, Richard: "Guantanamo Is Gulag of our Time, Says Amnesty." The Guardian, May 26 2005.

Ramsay, Dr Maureen: "Can the Torture of Terrorist Suspects Be Justified?" The International Journal of Human Rights, vol. 10, no. 2, 2006.

Sandberg, Britta: We Did Exactly what Al-Qaeda Wanted Us to Do. Der Speigel, Magazine, Sept 11 2011.

Serwer, Adam: Did General Petraeus Change His Position on Torture?" Washington Post, June 24 2011, Opinion pages

Shane, Scott: 9/11 May Have Been Stopped but for High-Level Dysfunction. New York Times, Sept 12 2011

Smith, Roger: The Taint of Torture Remains Despite overlay of Legal Process. Law Society Gazette ,Op-ed page May 17 2012

The Sun, front page headlined the Ricin Plot as a "Factory of Death." London, January 8 2003.

Warrick, Joby and Eggen, Dan: "Hill Briefed on Waterboarding in 2002." Washington Post, front page, Sunday, December 9, 2007.

WikiLeaks and other leaked classified documents

Department of Defense, Joint Task Force Guantanamo, marked secret// noforn//20300603. June 3 2005. Obtainable from the WikiLeaks website: http:// wikileaks.org/

MI6 letter, a copy of which was handed to the author of this dissertation in Tripoli. It was originally sent by fax to the office of Libya's then head of intelligence Musa Kusa. Simply marked: FOR THE URGENT AND PERSONAL ATTENTION OF MUSA KUSA, DEPARTMENT OF INTERNATIONAL RELATIONS AND COLLABORATION. March 18 2004. It was signed off by Sir Mark Allen, counter-terrorism chief.

SECONDARY SOURCES

Books

Alleg, Henri: The Question. Lincoln NE, University of Nebraska, Bison Books, 2006.

Allhoff, Fritz: Terrorism, Ticking Time-Bombs, and Torture. Chicago IL, University of Chicago Press, January 2012.

Aquinas, Thomas: The Summa Theologica. London, Burns Oates & Washbourne Ltd., May 1911.

Archer, Lawrence and Bawdon, Fiona: Ricin! The Inside Story of the Terror Plot that Never Was. London, Pluto Press, 2010.

Aussaresses, Paul: The Battle of the Casbah: Terrorism and Counter-Terrorism in Algeria, 1955–1957. New York, Enigma Books, 2002.

Bagaric, Mirko and Clarke, Julie: Torture. When the Unthinkable Is Morally Permissible, Albany NY, State University of New York Press, 2007.

Bates, Milton J. Reporting Vietnam Part Two: American Journalism 1969–1975. New York, The Library of America, 1998.

Begg, Moazzam: Enemy Combatant. London, Simon and Schuster UK Ltd., 2006.

Bergen, Peter: The Longest War: The Enduring Conflict between America and al-Qaeda. Free Press, 2011

Birley, Anthony R: Hadrian: The Restless Emperor. Routledge Publishing, 1997.

Blackler, John & Miller, Seumas: Ethical Issues in Policing. Ashgate, 2006

Blehm, Eric: The Only Thing Worth Dying For. New York, HarperCollins Publishers, 2010.

Brecher, Bob: Torture and the Ticking Bomb. Oxford, Blackwell Publishing, 2007.

Briley, John: Cry Freedom. London, Penguin, 1987.

Broadwell, Paula: All In. London, Penguin, 2012.

Campbell, John: Margaret Thatcher: The Iron Lady. London, Jonathan Cape, 2003.

Clausewitz, Von Carl: On War. Edited and translated by Michael Eliot Howard. Chichester, Princeton University Press, 1976.

Cobain, Ian: Cruel Britannia, London, Portobello Books, 2012.

Cole, David: The Torture Memos. New York, The New Press, 2009.

Dershowitz, Alan M: Why Terrorism Works: Understanding the Threat, Responding to the Challenge. New Haven and London, Yale University Press, 2002.

Farago, Ladislas: The Game of the Foxes. New York, David McKay Company, 1971.

Galula, David: Counterinsurgency Warfare: Theory and Practice. London, Praeger, 1964.

Gellman, Barton: Angler: The Cheney Vice Presidency. New York, Penguin Press, 2008.

Granger, Montgomery: Saving Grace at Guantanamo Bay. Durham CT, Strategic Book Publishing, 2010.

Greenberg, Karen J and Dratel, Joshua L: The Torture Papers, The Road to Abu Ghraib; Cambridge, Cambridge University Press 2005.

Gross, Michael L: Moral Dilemmas of Modern War. New York, Cambridge University Press, 2010.

Harbury, Jennifer K: Truth, Torture and the American Way. Boston, MA, Beacon Press, 2005.

Hayes, Stephen F: Cheney: The Untold Story of America's Most Powerful and Controversial Vice President. New York, HarperCollins, 2007.

Hillenbrand, Laura: Unbroken. London, Fourth Estate, 2010.

Hoare, Oliver: Camp 020, MI5 and the Nazi Spies. Public Record Office, Richmond, UK, 2000.

Howard, Michael, Andreopoulos, George J, Shulman, Mark R (eds.): The Laws of War: Constraints on Warfare in the Western World. New Haven CT, Yale University Press, 1994.

Hubbell, John G: P.O.W. New York, McGraw-Hill Book Company, 1976.

Kawczynski, Daniel: Seeking Gadaffi. Colorado Springs CO, Dialogue, 2011.

Kiriakou, John: The Reluctant Spy. New York, Bantam Books, 2009.

Lartéguy, Jean: The Centurions. Paris, Presses de la Cite, 1960.

Lazreg, Marnia: Torture and the Twilight of Empire – from Algiers to Baghdad. Princeton NJ, Princeton University Press, 2007.

Levinson, Stanford (ed.): Torture: A Collection. London, Oxford University Press, 2004.

Macintyre, Ben: Double Cross; The True Story of the D-Day Spies. London, Bloomsbury, 2012.

Manningham-Buller, Eliza: Securing Freedom. London, Profile Books, 2012.

Marlowe, Anne: David Galula: His Life and Intellectual Context. SSI Books, 2010

Mastors, Elena M: Breaking Al-Qaeda. Psychological and Operational Techniques. Washington DC, Library of Congress, 2010.

Mayer, Jane: The Dark Side: The Inside Story of How the War on Terror Turned into a War on American Ideals. Garden City NY, Doubleday, 2008.

McCoy, Alfred W: A Question of Torture: New York, Metropolitan Books, 2006.

McDermott, Terry and Meyer, Josh: The Hunt for KSM. New York, Little, Brown & Company, 2012.

McLean, Iain: Adam Smith, Radical and Egalitarian: An Interpretation for the 21st Century. Edinburgh, Edinburgh University Press, 2006.

McPhee, Peter: Robespierre – A Revolutionary Life. New Haven CT, Yale University Press, 2012.

Peirce, Gareth: Despatches from the Dark Side. On Torture and the Death of Justice. London, Verso, 2012.

Phillips, Joshua ES: None of Us Were Like this Before. American Soldiers and Torture. London, Verso, 2010.

Raday, Sophia: Love in a Condition Yellow: A Memoir of an Unlikely Marriage. Beacon Press, 2009.

Ridley, Yvonne: In the Hands of the Taliban. London, Robson Books, 2001.

Risen, James: State of War: The Secret History of the CIA and the Bush Administration. New York, Free Press, 2006.

Rousseau , Jacques J: The Confessions of Jean-Jacques Rousseau. London, Penguin Classics, 1973.

Sartre, Jean-Paul: No Exit and Three Other Plays. New York, Vintage International, 1989.

Scarry, Elaine: The Body in Pain. Oxford University Press, 1985.

Scheuer, Michael: Osama Bin Laden. New York, Oxford University Press, 2011.

Scheuer, Michael: Imperial Hubris: Why the West Is Losing the War on Terror. Dulles VA, Brassey's Inc., 2004.

Shawcross, William: Justice and the Enemy. Nuremberg, 9/11 and the Trial of Khalid Sheikh Mohammed. New York, Public Affairs, 2011.

Shecter, Cliff: The Real McCain. PoliPointPress, Sausalito CA, 2008.

Soufan, Ali: The Black Banners: The Inside Story of 9/11 and the War Against Al Qaeda. New York, W.W. Norton and Company, 2011.

Stephens, RWG: Camp 020, MI5 and the Nazi Spies. Public Records Office, Kew, 2000.

Taylor, Peter: Brits: The War Against the IRA. London, Bloomsbury, 2001

Trinquier, Roger: Modern Warfare: A French View of Counterinsurgency. Westport CT, Praeger Security International, 2006.

Tzu, Sun: The Art of War. Hollywood FL, Simon and Brown, 2010.

Vernon, J: The Illustrated History of Torture, from the Roman Empire to the War on Terror. London, Carlton Books, 2011.

Woods, Donald: Biko, London, Paddington Press, 1978.

Worthington, Andy: The Guantanamo Files: The Stories of 774 Detainees in America's Illegal Prison. Pluto Press 2007

Online Publications and Websites

ABC News: Ross, Brian and Esposito, Richard: "CIA's Harsh Interrogation Techniques Described." ABC News Investigative Unit, November 18 2005, ABC News. Accessed at http://abcnews.go.com/WNT/Investigation/story?id=1322866#.T1VP2ZhA4so.

Allhoff, Fritz website: http://www.allhoff.org/.

AFP News: Rabechault, Mathieu and De Luce, Dan: "Algeria Conflict Shapes US Military Strategy." March 14 2012. Accessed at http://www.google.com/hostednews/afp/article/ALeqM5iJSPQV_QY0WFuBQZ7aH3OCsGWeAw.

Aristotle: Nichomachean Ethics. The Internet Classics Archive. Accessed at http://classics.mit.edu//Aristotle/nicomachaen.html – Book 1 (9).

BBC, Newsnight: Ali Soufan reveals details of the interrogation of Zubaydah on September 12 2011: Footage, film and words can be accessed at http://www.bbc.co.uk/news/world-us-canada-14891439.

BBC News: Paul Reynolds reveals on website December 8 2005: "Defining Torture in a New World War." Accessed at http://news.bbc.co.uk/1/hi/4499528.stm.

Cageprisoners website: "Laa Tansa: Never Forget," launched January 10 2012, London, accessed at http://cageprisoners.com/our-work/events/item/3084-press-launch-laa-tansa-never-forget.

CNN.com/Law Center: Interview conducted by Wolf Blitzer.

Cooper, Michael and Santora, Marc: "McCain Rebukes Giuliani on Waterboarding Remark." New York Times, October 26 2007, accessed at http://www.nytimes.com/2007/10/26/us/politics/26giuliani.html?ref=politics#.

Department of Justice website: http://www.justice.gov/archive/ll/highlights.htm.

Danner, Mark: "The Red Cross Torture Report: What it Means." The New York Review of Books, p. 43, April 30 2009.

Demmer, Ulrike: "Rumsfeld Lawsuit Embarrasses German Authorities." Spiegel Online International, March 26 2007, accessed at http://www.spiegel.de/international/world/0,1518,473987,00.html.

Dershowitz, Alan M: "The Case Against Jordan." Jerusalem Post, October 9 2003, reproduced in several online publications, including Frontpagemag.com.

Duff, Gordon: "Military and Foreign Affairs Journal: Bush 'Blood Money' Tour Cancelled." Veteran's Today, Feb 6 2011, accessed at http://www.veteranstoday.com/2011/02/06/gordon-duff-bush-blood-money-tour-cancelled/.

Finn, Peter: "Detainee Who Gave False Iraq Data Dies in Prison in Libya." Washington Post online, May 12 2009, accessed at http://www.webcitation.org/query?url=http%3A%2F%2Fwww.allgov.com%2FViewNews%2FSource_for_Colin_Powells_Fake_UN_Claim_of_Iraq_al_Qaeda_Connection_Dies_in_Libyan_Prison_90513&date=May.

The Guardian newspaper report: http://www.theguardian.com/uk-news/2016/may/31/revealed-britain-rendition-policy-rift-between-spy-agencies-mi6-mi5

Hastings, Michael: "The Runaway General." Rolling Stone, p. 1108–1109, July 8–22 2010, on newsstands Friday, June 25. Accessed at http://www.rollingstone.com/politics/news/the-runaway-general-20100622#ixzz1pZeQkdyU.

Le Monde Newspaper and archives: "L'accablante Confession du Général Aussaresses sur la Torture en Algérie." Le Monde, May 3 2001, accessed at Le Monde online archives: http://www.lemonde.fr/cgi-bin/ACHATS/acheter.cgi?offre=ARCHIVES&type_item=ART_ARCH_30J&objet_id=702899#.

Levin, Carl: "New Report: Bush Officials Tried to Shift Blame for Detainee Abuse to Low-Ranking Soldiers." Huffington Post, April 21 2009, accessed at http://www.huffingtonpost.com/sen-carl-levin/new-report-bush-officials_b_189823.html.

Miller, Greg: "John Rizzo: The Most Influential Career Lawyer in CIA History." Los Angeles Times, Feature Section, June 29 2009, accessed at http://articles.latimes.com/2009/jun/29/nation/na-cia-lawyer29.

Oxford Dictionaries Online is a free site offering a comprehensive dictionary, grammar guidance, puzzles and games and a language blog. Online reference for torture accessed at http://oxforddictionaries.com/definition/torture.

Raday, Sophia: "David Petraeus Wants this French Novel Back in Print!" Slate online magazine, January 27 2011, accessed at http://www.slate.com/id/2282462/.

Shakir, Faiz: "McCain Calls Waterboarding 'A Horrible Torture Technique,' But Will He Vote Against Mukasey?" Think Progress Security website; October 26 2007, accessed at http://thinkprogress.org/security/2007/10/26/17210/mccain-mukasey-torture/.

Shenon, Philip: "Panel Pushes Nominee to Denounce Technique." New York Times, October 24 2007, accessed at http://www.nytimes.com/2007/10/24/washington/24mukasey.html?ref=us.

U.S. Army Field Manuals: accessed at http://www.loc.gov/rr/frd/Military_Law/pamphlets_manuals.html.

The White House government website: accessed at http://www.whitehouse.gov/the_press_office/EnsuringLawfulInterrogations.

Williams, David: "CIA Ran Secret 'Ghost Prisons' for Terror Suspects in Europe." Daily Mail, June 8 2007, accessed at http://www.dailymail.co.uk/news/article-460749/CIA-ran-secret-ghost-prisons-terror-suspects-Europe.html.

Television News, Documentaries and TV Series

ABC News: John Kiriakou, a 15-year veteran of the agency's intelligence analysis and operations directorates, sparked a national debate in the US over torture in December 2007 when he told ABC's Brian Ross and Richard Esposito that senior al-Qaeda commando Abu Zubaydah became confessional after one waterboarding.

BBC, Newsnight: Ali Soufan reveals details of the interrogation of Zubaydah on September 12 2011: Footage, film and words can be accessed at http://www.bbc.co.uk/news/world-us-canada-14891439.

CNN presents documentary "Dead Wrong – Inside an Intelligence Meltdown." August 21 2005. CNN Online reference accessed at http://edition.cnn.com/2005/WORLD/meast/08/19/powell.un/index.html, August 23 2005.

Fox News: "24" was produced for the network and syndicated worldwide. Premiering on November 6 2001, the show spanned 192 episodes over eight seasons, with the series finale broadcast on May 24 2010.

PBS: Transcript and 28-minute-long video of the Frontline documentary, "The Interrogator." Accessed at http://www.pbs.org/wgbh/pages/frontline/the-interrogator/ on September 13 2011.

Cinema and DVD/Video releases

"Guantanamo: Inside the Wire". A Documentary by David Miller. Journeyman Pictures, 2009.

"Lost Command." DVD, 2002, a 1966 war film directed by Mark Robson and filmed in Spain. The screenplay was written by Nelson Gidding, based on the 1960 novel The Centurions by Jean Lartéguy.

Index

Lightning Source UK Ltd.
Milton Keynes UK
UKOW05f2115020916

281992UK00006B/181/P